RETHINKING

RISK

How Companies Sabotage Themselves and
What They Must Do Differently

JOSEPH W. KOLETAR

ΛMACOM

American Management Association

New York • Atlanta • Brussels • Chicago • Mexico City • San Francisco
Shanghai • Tokyo • Toronto • Washington, D.C.

Bulk discounts available. For details visit:
www.amacombooks.org/go/specialsales
Or contact special sales:
Phone: 800-250-5308
Email: specialsls@amanet.org
View all the AMACOM titles at: www.amacombooks.org

This publication is designed to provide accurate and
authoritative information in regard to the subject matter
covered. It is sold with the understanding that the publisher is
not engaged in rendering legal, accounting, or other
professional service. If legal advice or other expert assistance is
required, the services of a competent professional person should
be sought.

Library of Congress Cataloging-in-Publication Data

Koletar, Joseph W.
  Rethinking risk : how companies sabotage themselves and what they must do differently /
Joseph W. Koletar.
      p.   cm.
  Includes bibliographical references and index.
  ISBN-13: 978-0-8144-1496-5
  ISBN-10: 0-8144-7353-9
  1. Risk management.   2. Fraud—Prevention.   3. Employee crimes—Prevention.   I. Title.
HD61.K626   2010
658.15′5—dc22

                                                                      2009052200

About AMA

American Management Association (www.amanet.org. is a world leader in talent development,
advancing the skills of individuals to drive business success. Our mission is to support the goals
of individuals and organizations through a complete range of products and services, including
classroom and virtual seminars, webcasts, webinars, podcasts, conferences, corporate and
government solutions, business books and research. AMA's approach to improving performance
combines experiential learning—learning through doing—with opportunities for ongoing
professional growth at every step of one's career journey.

Printing number

10   9   8   7   6   5   4   3   2   1

This book is dedicated to the
three great institutions that shaped my life:
the Pennsylvania State University,
the United States Army,
and the Federal Bureau of Investigation.

CONTENTS

AUTHOR'S NOTE

. . . .

Please read this section. It will help you better appreciate and utilize what I am going to present.

Allow me to explain, for your benefit, what this book is not. After that, I will explain what it is. This book is not an anthology of "risk." Were I to cover even the various aspects of financial risk, the book would be at least three times as long as it is, and I doubt very many would find it of interest. There are easily hundreds of books, professional organizations, and vendors that deal with financial risk. And that does not begin to deal with the hundreds of other forms of risk that can affect a corporation. For example, I also do not cover issues involving competitive risk (how to protect yourself or prepare for a potential new competitor who suddenly appears and takes away all your business); regulatory risk (how to ensure or prepare for new regulations that alter the landscape and destroy or diminish your business; legal risk (e.g., how to protect yourself from litigious employees through detailed employee handbooks); and intellectual property risk (how to avoid losing intellectual property or proprietary competitive advantages). A book designed to cover all of those would be the size of your car, or perhaps your house.

Risk, be it personal, professional, or in business, is a fact of life. Merely crossing the street in the everyday course of events entails some element of risk, but we accept it without question for a number of reasons: we want to get to the other side of the street; we have done it many times before without harm or incident; we take prudent precautions (e.g., look both ways). Yet, once we enter the realm of business or organizational boundaries, something changes. We understand that risk exists, and we have an inherent instinct and obligation to acknowledge its presence. Accordingly, we often build elaborate defenses against it and employ powerful devices (usually computers) to detect and prevent it. Yet, at the same time, we frequently suffer two consequences of our actions. On the one hand, we are deluged with copious (and often useless) data, and on the other we are still subject to the sudden shock of events unforeseen.

How, in an age of powerful machines capable of producing data faster than we can interpret and absorb it, are we still failing to deal intelligently and effectively with risk? How, with all the sophisticated information reporting systems available today, can one unscrupulous employee bring down a 300-year-old blue-chip bank such as Barings?

Fraud is perhaps the best-known form of risk, since it gets so much attention from the media, from regulators, and from the public. It is instructive, since the operative principles that drive it propel most forms of risk. I believe that what applies for fraud risk applies for all kinds of risk. This book is mostly a discussion about fraud, but I will show that preventing and detecting fraud requires a risk management mindset as well as risk management processes that can help the company better manage all kinds of risk.

I try to focus on some of the key principles and mistakes I have seen in more than forty years spent dealing with risk in all its many and varied forms. I think these insights will be of value to board members, audit committee members, "C suite" executives, middle managers, auditors, investors, educators, students, and others. I have traveled the highway of risk many times and seen it in its many forms. I hope that my experience and ruminations will be of some value, for over the years I have come to some conclusions. Whatever the nature of a particular risk may be, there seem to me to be recurring themes, common mistakes, faulty judgments that appear with regularity. Given that I have worked in scores of industries, it strikes me that perhaps exploring these issues will be of value to those interested in risk, regardless of its particular type or nature.

Some unusual ideas and theories may result from this effort, and I make no apologies for them. I have seen enough financial loss, organizational disruption, and human suffering to convince me that we could probably do a better job managing risk.

To some degree, this book is about our "philosophy" of risk—how we think of it, conceptualize it, and deal with it. I think this is important, for it dictates all our other actions—the theories of risk we embrace, the tools and techniques we utilize, and so on. Without giving thought to our basic philosophical construct, we are adrift, to be steered by the impulse or "tool" of the moment.

This book, for ease of understanding, generally uses the terms "corporation" and "corporate." However, the issues set forth apply to all organizations, be they publicly traded companies, privately held entities, not-for-profits, or governmental units. Risk, like fraud, is universal, and the principles and lessons learned apply universally, as well.

When attempting to deal with "risk," one faces a daunting task, as the field is so large. Information technology (IT) dominates a good deal of the literature, as IT plays so important a role in gathering, organizing, coordinating, integrating, and displaying the data needed to make informed decisions about risk in its many and varied forms. Likewise, there are a number of techniques and processes that are designed to help the organization better define its objectives and marshal its resources to achieve them. Probably among the most popular are the Six Sigma[1] and Balanced Scorecard[2] techniques that have grown to almost mythological proportions in organizational literature.

This book approaches the subject from a somewhat different perspective, that of the human dimension. In the history of the world, a computer has never stolen a cent or caused any serious corporate problem. Certainly, like any other machine, computers can fail, but more often they "fail" because of the information that was fed into them, the assumptions they were told to make, or the way that information was interpreted. Can they be used by the unscrupulous for nefarious purposes? Certainly, much in the same way that a knife or a screwdriver can, but it is the people element, in my experience, that is the most important.

To some small degree, I am going to try to teach you to think like a "cop." I do not use that term in any negative or demeaning way, as, from the small-town police officer to the most elite federal agents, we are all "cops," and, having been one, I have the greatest respect for them and what they do. All they deal with is risk. Some small percentage of the time, it is their own risk (you can get hurt or killed doing these things), but 95 percent of the time it is your risk—your risk of being killed, raped, assaulted, of having your property stolen, or of having something bad happen to your kids.

They have been doing this a long time, and they have become rather good at it. Perfect, no, but good, yes. We can learn much from them, so you will see some law enforcement references in this book.

Do not be put off by them. I spent twenty-five years in law enforcement (at the FBI) and worked with many fine agencies, whether local, county, state, or federal. I have also spent fifteen years in the private sector, and believe there is much to be learned from what the "cops" can tell us.

In thinking about the human element of risk, we can learn much from the tragic events of 9/11. Following this disaster, any number of investigations were initiated, any number of hearings held, and more than a few commissions convened. Good, intelligent, and hard-working people spent many hours, days, and months examining the incidents and the circumstances that led up to them. Two of the more frequent themes coming out of these inquiries had to do with "connecting the dots" and HUMINT.

"Connecting the dots" refers to the need to pull all relevant information together in a timely manner so as to be able to make better-informed assessments and decisions. As noted in this book, this happens too infrequently in corporations, for a variety of reasons.

For those not familiar with the world of intelligence, usually called the Intelligence Community (IC in the business), it has its own language. In that community, HUMINT (human intelligence) shares space with ELINT (electronic intelligence), SIGINT (signals intelligence), COMINT (communications intelligence), and much more. HUMINT, put in the most simple of terms, refers to spies and "sources," as they are known. These are people who, for reasons of ideology, money, fear of retribution, or desire to change teams, are willing to talk about what is going on and to provide useful, even vital information on personalities, agendas, plans, rivalries, and weaknesses. In the IC community this is crucial information to know. Many of the findings of the post-9/11 era were that, while the United States had excelled in the "technical means of collection" (e.g., satellites surveying areas of interest, computers analyzing data collected through other "technical means"), we were weak in the field of HUMINT—the people side of the equation. Again, to relate this to corporate risk, too often corporations get into trouble because they do not fully utilize the "HUMINT" available to them.[3]

To some degree, this is the situation we find ourselves in with regard to corporate risk. We seem to excel at creating, packaging, and distributing data, but we often find ourselves (or so many of my clients tell me) lacking in solid information or, as some prefer, "actionable intelligence." I will try to offer some suggestions, based on my client work, to change that situation.

Much of this book is written in the first person, as I talk about what I have seen in more than forty years of dealing with risk. While I spent twenty-seven years in the federal government, I later spent fifteen years in the private sector dealing with corporate risk, including time spent at Fortune 10 companies. The similarities between the governmental and the private sectors are striking because, again, risk is universal. I have seen risk in just about every industry, from waste management to nuclear power. I have seen what can go wrong, found out why it went wrong, and made recommendations to lessen its likelihood in the future.

While I have interviewed experts and read widely in preparing this book, a fair amount of what I recount pertains to my experience in dealing with corporate fraud and security issues. These are quite common forms of risk, and fraud in particular seems to have a knack of finding the front page of the newspapers or being the lead item in the electronic media. From Enron to Bernie Madoff, it seems to be everywhere. At the same time, we can learn from it and apply the lessons we learn broadly, whatever our field and whatever the nature of the particular risks we face in our corporate lives.

I have had the benefit of dealing with many risk professionals throughout my careers. Some are colleagues, and many are friends. They have been invariably generous in sharing their stories, knowledge, and recollections. In this book, I try to provide a menu that includes not only what I have seen and believe I have learned but also the collective wisdom these colleagues possess regarding risk in its various forms and in how it appears in many industries. I think you will find their stories interesting and, with a little imagination, will be able to translate them to help you deal with whatever form of risk you face in your professional life.

A number of these insights come from professionals with whom I worked in the FBI. The FBI itself is a great learning environment, but these folks, relying on their skills and their work ethic, often went on to highly successful careers in the private sector following retirement, in a variety of pursuits. I am thankful for their insights.

Risk is a difficult thing to talk about and, therefore, research. Paradoxically, there is risk in even talking about risk. I gave all of my interviewees a choice between being fully identified and having the name of their current or former employer mentioned and remaining anonymous. Some respondents picked one or the other, and others chose not to participate, for they feared that the repercussions of discussion and disclosure, even after they had left an employer, might be too great. To those who chose to participate, I am grateful; to those who did not, I understand. Risk is a risky business.

In social science research, this is referred to as a "double blind" phenomenon: not only is the topic risky, but even talking about it is risky. Thus, much experience and useful information remain hidden from public view. My intent in this book is to peel back that cover a bit and expose what I have learned for the possible benefit of those inclined to look.

The reader will note that some chapters are longer than others. There is a reason for this. Throughout my career, I mainly dealt with "train wrecks," as you will see in the introduction that follows. Thus, I tend to know a lot about what can go wrong and how it went wrong and why pretty smart people did not see it coming. May their stories be instructive.

Throughout this text, for those who wished to be identified, I provide names and corporate affiliations. To shield those who were willing to provide information and insights but did not wish to be publicly identified, I have provided fictitious names for them and for their companies. I hope you understand.

A final word of caution; this is not a "happy" book. If you want to listen to "Everything Is Beautiful," go elsewhere. I spent my several careers dealing with problems. I have seen what can go wrong and have been called in to investigate and explain it. If you believe in learning from the mistakes of others, as opposed to trying to emulate their successes, please read on. I think you will find it of value.

NOTES

1. There are any number of books on this technique, which has been around for decades. A place to start is Thomas Pyzdek, *The Six Sigma Handbook: The Complete Guide for Greenbelts, Blackbelts, and Managers at All Levels* (New York: McGraw-Hill, 2003).
2. Robert S. Kaplan and David P. Morton, *The Balanced Scorecard* (New York: Norton, 1996). This is but one of several works on the technique.
3. For an exhaustive exploration of these issues, see *The 9/11 Commission Report: Final Report of The National Commission on Terrorist Attacks upon the United States* (New York: Norton, 2003).

ACKNOWLEDGMENTS

It would be very difficult to produce a book on a topic as broad and complex as risk without the help of many people. While any errors or omissions are solely my responsibility, I am deeply grateful for their assistance, knowledge, and insights.

As always, thanks to my lovely wife, Martha, who puts up with me and guides me through the world of computers and other mysterious machines.

Others whom I must recognize include:

First, my friend and publisher, Hank Kennedy, of AMACOM, the publishing arm of the American Management Association. Hank is wise, supportive, and, best of all, funny.

Second, my friend and colleague Joe Wells, the founder of the Association of Certified Fraud Examiners. In the space of twenty years, some hard-working people have built a successful business. Very few have built a profession, thereby enriching the lives of thousands and bringing much-needed assistance to corporations and organizations around the world. Joe has done that.

Others to whom I am deeply indebted include:

Dr. Ed Delattre, the former dean of one college and the departmental dean of another, as well as the world's leading authority on law enforcement ethics, frequent lecturer at the FBI Academy, prolific author, frequent speaker, long-time corporate board member, severe critic of what he sees as the shortcomings of American higher education, and all-around nice guy;

Dean Hank Foley, of the School of Information Sciences and Technology at the Pennsylvania State University, who is leading that fine school into the future;

Ken Friedman, seasoned corporate attorney and man about town in the tonier areas of Manhattan;

Edward "Fast Eddie" Gartner, of Shallotte, North Carolina, the "car guy";

Trent Gazzaway, national practice leader for the international professional services firm Grant Thornton LLP and dedicated professional in the area of corporate governance;

Grace Ghezzi, my colleague from the Association of Certified Fraud Examiners and one of the stars of the field;

John Gilmartin, retired assistant chief of the New York Police Department (NYPD), who, in addition to being a "computer guy," has seen law enforcement at every level, from the street to NYPD Headquarters;

Peter Hoffman, retired group managing partner of Deloitte & Touche LLP (D&T), who took a chance on hiring a "Fed" out of the FBI fifteen years ago and who, in his career, has seen just about everything that can go wrong in a corporation;

Sheriff John W. Ingram V, Lieutenant Joe Scoggins, and Detective Sergeant Steve Mason of the Brunswick County (NC) Sheriff's Office, dedicated public servants all;

Professor Ed Ketz, of the Pennsylvania State University;

Skip Lange, my old buddy and a gifted and well-traveled consultant;

Chris Mansuy, my friend for more than forty years and a talented maritime attorney on Wall Street;

Dr. Daven Morrison, a young, energetic, talented, and insightful psychiatrist practicing in the greater Chicago area who, with his father, Dr. David Morrison, has done yeoman work on executive behavior in corporations;

Bill Parrett, my old boss, who led an already great firm, Deloitte & Touche LLP, to even greater heights and who remained a nice guy in the process;

Dr. Sri Ramamoorti, CPA, educator, researcher, scholar, prolific author, member of many professional boards and societies, past and present colleague, partner at Grant Thornton LLP, and a valued friend;

Henry Ristuccia, head of D&T's governance and risk management practice and a trusted and experienced advisor to corporations throughout the world;

Tom Sheer, retired assistant director of the FBI, corporate executive, my boss on several occasions, and my friend;

Cecil Sherman, a long-time family friend who knows more about the retail business and internal controls than anyone else I ever met;

Jim Thomas, who built one college from the ground up at the Pennsylvania State University and is now the dean of its Smeal College of Business, a gracious host and a fun companion, in addition to being a visionary;

Dave Vannort, a long-time partner at Deloitte & Touche LLP, a former compliance officer, and an all-around nice guy;

Fred Verinder, my friend and former colleague, who always lived up to his nickname, Freddie the Fabulous Federal Ferret.

Finally, I'd like to thank Don Barnes, my friend for more than forty years and a prominent attorney in Washington, D.C., and Bob Hack, a corporate sleuth of the first order, who never saw an issue he could not figure out.

INTRODUCTION

"People don't call us because they're having a great day."

Anonymous

This is an accepted mantra in my business, along with "Did you ever hear of anybody stealing a million dollars and working their way down?"

I have spent more than forty-two years dealing with various forms of risk, and along the way I have seen more than a few things. I also learned a few lessons through the bitter experience of others.

Organizational problems are a fact of life, and few of them get smaller with time. Once a problem develops, it tends to grow, usually until it is too large to hide; then, one day, the organization senses it, goes into a panic mode, and picks up the phone.

When asked what I do for a living, I often jokingly reply, "Fix train wrecks."

Unfortunately, that's pretty much all I see—train wrecks. I am sure the vast majority of corporations and organizations work just fine, but please be assured that a fair amount of time they do not. Otherwise, I, and thousands of people like me, would be out of work.

The purpose of this book is not to increase the amount of work we get. Believe me, there is more than enough in the pipeline. The objective is to help organizations do a better job of sensing and dealing with problems before they get too big. Ideally, corporations would prevent problems from developing in the first place. This is, to use the more general term, risk mitigation.

I have seen the scene hundreds of times. It does not matter what the name of the company is, what industry it is in, or how big or small it may be; it is always the same. You enter the conference room, and there they are, huddled around the table: the "C suite" executives, the general counsel, the outside counsel, probably someone from internal audit and the compliance function, and perhaps someone from human resources. They always look the same—confused, shocked, angry, worried, and anxious. Usually, the problem has been through the first round of analysis, and the preliminary findings have been discussed. The lawyers have weighed in with their initial thoughts on the legal and regulatory issues that may be involved. Now they want to know what to do. How to answer the basic questions:

How did this happen?

How big is it?

Who did it?

Occasionally, "Is this an isolated incident?"

Rarely, "How do we prevent this in the future?"

This book is an attempt to answer the last question. If we can answer that, we need not worry about the first four.

The idea for this book, which had been perking for a while, came to me in February 2008.

My wife and I, along with several of our neighbors, were on an eleven-day cruise through the Caribbean, with stops in Costa Rica and Panama. For me, the highlight of the trip was our passage through the Panama Canal. I had always wanted to see it, and it surpassed all my expectations.

As our huge cruise ship cleared the first lock, we docked, and various groups disembarked for day trips. My wife and I chose a trip on an opened-sided boat that offered a detailed tour of the canal. Our tour guides had been doing this for years, and they provided numerous facts and tidbits about the building and operation of the canal.

As we proceeded, we passed a number of other ships heading in the opposite direction. Several of them were massive container cargo vessels, almost 1,000 feet long and capable of carrying thousands of containers.

As one passed, one of the guides drew our attention to the stern of the vessel. There, hanging from a davit, was a solitary lifeboat. The guide explained that it took about twenty people to operate that large and complex a vessel.

That was my "Eureka" moment. "Holy mackerel," I thought. "That's only about six people a shift!"

My mind flashed to corporate train wrecks, which are always a failure of corporate controls, and I thought: "If container ships can achieve this level of control efficiency, why can't the modern corporation?"

Obviously, I use "container ships" and "dashboard metrics" in a somewhat loose manner. Dashboard metrics are at once both simple and complex. The concept has been around a number of years, and many excellent consultants and companies have tried to develop and implement them. The premise is simple: can we design the monitoring and control systems of a large, complex organization so that the data flow will detect what is important or out of acceptable boundaries and cause it to show up on the "dashboard" of a "C suite" executive, much like the "check engine soon" panel on your car flashes when you need to attend to something?

So, too, with container ships. I spent two years in the Army as an intelligence officer during the Vietnam War. I know nothing about ships, but I know some people who do. One was Chris Mansuy, a fraternity brother and a lifelong friend, who for almost four decades has been a highly successful maritime lawyer on Wall Street. Before that, he spent four years as a naval officer. Surely he would know more than I did, so I called him. He listened to my thesis and replied simply, "It's mainly dead space."

He was right. While they are huge vessels, container ships contain mainly cargo. If you have good control systems, it's fairly easy to keep track of what is going on. So too when I posed my question to a colleague who is a computer executive with the aerospace company, Lockheed Martin. He also replied simply: "They got rid of the people."

What he meant was: automated systems can do a very efficient job of monitoring "dead" space.

That is all well and good, but the vast majority of organizations are full of the most productive, innovative, energetic, and troublesome creatures on the face of the earth—people. In many cases, the people working to prevent risk will discover that the cause of risk is other people—people taking shortcuts or people engaged in outright fraud.

How do we attempt to monitor people's activities, good or bad, productive or unproductive, without trying to establish a prison camp? (For what it is worth, having spent the better part of three decades in law enforcement, I can tell you that prisons themselves are notoriously unruly places, and these guys live in steel cages.)

This is the challenge we face when we think of controls in general and risk mitigation in particular. How do we do it? How do we establish systems and procedures that give us some level of assurance that we know what is going on?

The veteran news anchor Tom Brokaw was a guest on the *Morning Joe* television show on MSNBC on December 26, 2008 (at 5:30 A.M.). The discussion was around the governmental and corporate financial mess in which the United States found itself. Brokaw is an old dog. He has been around the block more than a few times, and he has pretty much seen it all. He replied, simply: "The guys at the top didn't know what was going on."

This is what happens in corporations so often, and it is a tragic mistake in several ways. First, the consequences are severe. Great institutions can fall in a matter of days or weeks, ruining careers, losing fortunes, and altering pension plans forever. Second, and most tragic, is that it does not have to happen. "Knowing what's going on" is neither terribly expensive nor unnecessarily complex. Much of it is common sense, and most of the data required are already available; they just have not been properly organized nor had enough attention paid to them. Addressing these weaknesses is neither outrageously expensive nor complicated, but it does take some effort. The work of half a dozen smart, dedicated people can make a huge difference in the risk assessment environment of a corporation.

This is not exclusively a "C suite" issue, although a good bit of the responsibility falls there. The "C suite" executives must operate off the information they receive (there is a huge difference between "data" and "information," and we will explore that in detail). Oversight, monitoring, and ensuring the integrity of information are the responsibility of all of management, be it senior, midlevel, or shop-floor. If management fails anywhere along the line, bad things often happen.

While a corporation or institution can fall with shocking suddenness once its problems become public, this does not have to happen. The issues that brought the company down did not happen overnight. They built slowly but steadily and were there for all to see, if anyone had chosen to look. This is the third, and arguably the greatest, tragedy. Why did we not take the time to look? Are we like the person who has a physical ailment but chooses not to go to a doctor lest he receive bad news?

My friend and colleague Dr. Ed Delattre has worn many hats throughout his career. He is the leading authority in the world on law enforcement ethics, and at least one of his books, *Character and Cops*, is now in its fifth printing.[1] He has also been the dean of one college and a department dean at another. He is a long-time corporate director and a much-sought-after speaker. We have, over the years, had many interesting and instructive discussions, either in person or on the telephone. Ed is a fierce critic of much of what he sees in the current educational system in the United States. As might be expected, his views are not always welcome, however sound they may be in fact.

We once had a lengthy conversation about the state of education in the United States, and Ed made a rather subtle, but profound, observation. Beginning in the 1950s, there was a shift in the academic world. Professors, until that time, primarily identified with their colleges or universities. But, at mid-century, the process of identification began to shift. Professors began to identify more with their field than with the institution they served. Papers were published, books were written, professional associations were joined, and career opportunities were examined. Thus was born mobility. Today, it is not unusual for a "star" professor to leave one school for another, sometimes taking much of her department with her. Salary and prestige are the coin of the realm.

The same phenomenon is now evident in other fields. Even old, "white shoe" law firms are not immune, as top-producing attorneys, and sometimes their entire practices, defect one day to what they see as greener pastures.

Several years ago, at a meeting of the National Association of Corporate Directors, John Bogle, the visionary investor who founded the Vanguard family of mutual funds, made an enlightening presentation. He had statistics readily at hand, but his message was simple: we have become a nation of traders rather than investors. We buy a stock, hoping for a quick profit, then sell and move on to the next stock. We have no long-term interest in the health of the company we invested in or in how well its corporate governance and risk management systems are working.

We see this today in corporate America. Failed CEOs jump from one company to another, facing no apparent consequences arising from their poor track records at their most recent employers. Indeed, they usually land softly, aided by a "golden parachute."

The logical conclusion here is that because fewer people identify with an institution (company, university) than was previously the case, they don't care as much about how well it is run and therefore don't take "the time to look."

Trying to compress more than forty years of professional experience into a little over 300 pages is a risk in and of itself. I have encountered those in the past who accuse me of "telling war stories." Perhaps I do, but that is how I learned. I certainly learned in more formal settings, in the course of pursuing several graduate degrees, and from the research needed to produce numerous professional articles, books, and speeches, but what tends to stick in my head are the scenes I saw firsthand. Actually, these are case studies, and my role, in social science research terms, was that of a "participant-observer." I was present and took an active role, but in this book I am trying to step back and recount what I learned that may be of benefit to others.

This book is largely about the mistakes of well-intentioned, intelligent people who made the wrong assumptions, or trusted the wrong people, or did not understand their corporate environment as well as they thought they did. These episodes persist and resonate, because, if we are not attentive, they could happen to any of us. I use "war stories" because they are sticky—you tend to remember a scene and a story better than you remember a management axiom.

NOTE

1. Edwin J. Delattre, *Character and Cops: Ethics in Policing* (Washington, D.C.: American Enterprise Institute for Public Policy Research, 2005).

RETHINKING

RISK

1.

· ·

OBSERVATIONS ABOUT RISK

· · · · · · · · · · · · · · · · · · ·

Risk surrounds us. Indeed, to a large degree, it defines us as human beings.

This chapter may come across as a bit philosophical, but this is done for a reason. Much of the damage that I have seen risk produce was not the result of a lack of intelligence or an indifference to its possibility. Those who suffered did so not for a lack of available help. Professional and commercial associations abound to assist in risk identification and mitigation, and legions of consultants, big and small, are ready to respond on short notice. The failures I have seen and dealt with came much more often from the psychological and perceptual attitudes adopted toward dealing with risk.

A useful and insightful definition of risk can be gleaned from one of the leading books in the world on internal auditing. It sets forth this definition:

Risk management, which is closely interlinked with governance, is the process conducted by management to understand and deal with the uncertainties (i.e., risks and opportunities) that could affect the organization's ability to achieve its objectives.[1]

THE MANY FACES OF RISK

In thinking about so large a topic, it is necessary to limit the scope of the discussion, lest it wander all over the map. Many years ago, the noted theorist John Rohr noted the same issue with regard to another important, but broad, topic—ethics:

> It will come as a surprise to no one to learn that the field of ethics is chaotic. The term is undefined; the inquiry unbounded. . . . I find myself looking for reasons to cut the topic back to manageable proportions.[2]

This book is about organizational risk. Certainly, there is more than enough personal risk to go around—illness, job loss, the breakup of a relationship, accidents—but organizational risk presents some interesting and special challenges. Few organizations reward employees for avoiding or minimizing risk. They want to see production, sales, and bottom-line results. In addition, risk is tricky to measure, and we tend to like things we can easily measure. An order for $20,000 is better than an order for $15,000. But how much risk did you, by virtue of your hard work and diligence, prevent today? That is a much more difficult scorecard to keep.

Think of any corporate performance plan you have ever had, regardless of your level or position in your organization. Typically, in my experience, there are one or two metrics—for example, sales and production—that are pretty easily measured. There are usually other elements to the plan that are supposedly co-equal, such as mentoring less-senior staff people or using technology wisely, but in reality these do not count for much. If you have a year where your performance was stellar in every other area but your sales performance was poor, it doesn't take much imagination to figure out what will happen.

Then consider risk mitigation. This phrase rarely appears in performance plans, and, even in the rare instances when it does, mitigation is difficult to measure.

Yet, for all it elusiveness, risk comes in a dizzying variety of forms. A corporation may face litigation, financial, competitive, environmental, foreign exchange, political, labor, technological, strategic, ethical, or intellectual risk. And this list could easily be expanded. In their desire to reduce labor and thereby unit costs, many corporations have moved some elements of their production operations to low-cost countries (LCC). This seems to work well, but it also comes with attendant elements of risk. Too many corporations have come to rue the day their name appeared on the front page of a newspaper that has broken a story about the use of child labor abroad, slave-like working conditions, or the use of lead-based paint or other contaminants in consumer products.

WHO OWNS RISK?

Then there is the issue of ownership. In most corporations, it is pretty obvious who is responsible for sales, and those folks get rewarded or sanctioned according to some fairly clear guidelines. But, who "owns" risk? Is it the board of directors, the audit committee, the chief executive officer, the chief financial officer, or someone else? Where exactly does it nest? Very few corporations have chief risk officers, and even those that do still have some problems with which to deal.

A good friend of mine, Ken Friedman (whom I quote later in this book), has spent his life as a corporate attorney in New York City. When presented with the question about who owns risk, he responded in his usual funny, sardonic, but insightful manner: "Until something goes wrong, nobody owns it. When the train goes off the tracks, everybody owns it."

He is right, in more ways than one. When a significant negative event impacts a corporation, there is more than enough risk to go around. The board of directors is worried that it will be criticized for not providing effective oversight. The audit committee will be pushing the internal and external auditors to explain how they could have missed what now appears to be so plainly in sight. The board will be pushing the "C suite" executives to explain why they allowed this to happen. The "C suite" executives will be hammering senior management as to why it did not have better controls in place. Senior management will be on top of middle management as to why it did not see the issue coming, and middle management will be probing lower-level supervisors about why needed information was not produced early enough to permit protective action. Shareholders will be calling the investor relations department, fearful of the impact of the event on their financial positions, and the media will be circling to see if there is a story here, perhaps even a series of stories, or, better yet, stories that can be linked to corporate missteps elsewhere. Legislators may convene hearings, and regulators will become focused. Lower-level employees will be worried about losing their jobs, and productivity will suffer. Customers will become antsy, and vendors will begin to wonder if they are going to get paid. Plaintiffs' attorneys, ever vigilant, will be considering possible causes of action.

When risk hits, it hits everyone, and it sometimes hits hard.

POSITIVE AND NEGATIVE RISK

Yet, for all of this, risk is a multifaceted thing. There is negative risk, as described, but there is also positive risk—risks associated with a new product line, a new ad campaign, a new acquisition or joint venture. The list could go on, but risk is in many ways the essence of business. Those who can handle it will prosper, and those that cannot will fail or stagnate.

This point was perhaps never as well made as in the old television show *The Twilight Zone*. On the air from 1959 to 1964, it was years ahead of its time and presented an array of human issues and foibles in a serious but entertaining way. One show in particular concerned an inveterate gambler. His compulsion was so bad that it had cost him his job and his family. As he wandered the city with but a few dollars left in his pocket, he was struck by a cab while crossing the street. When he awoke, he felt fine and looked around to find himself in a casino. Taking the money he had left, he began to gamble. He won. He continued to gamble, trying one game after another. He won. He could not lose and concluded from the little he could remember of the accident that he was in Heaven. As the evening wore on, the realization began to set in that he was, in fact, in Hell. For a gambler, a world without risk is no world at all.

So, too, with those of us in more mainstream lines of pursuit. A football game without another team on the field would not be much fun to watch. We enjoy competition and the thrill of a hard-earned victory, and we accept the element of risk that comes with competition. However, this is positive risk. Negative risk is another matter entirely, and if we are prudent we will take all reasonable steps to avoid it. But we often do not. One need only scan the headlines to see evidence of corporate failure almost every day. The run of financial misstatement issues in what is now called the "Enron" era is legendary, and this era has now been replaced by the "Madoff" era.

It began with corporate failures on Wall Street, followed by the implosion of quasi-governmental institutions like Freddie Mac and Fannie Mae, capped off with what appears to have been a massive, decades-long Ponzi scheme run by financier Bernard Madoff that lured in some of the "best and the brightest." Untold billions were lost, retirements were wiped out, careers were shattered, charities and universities had to curtail operations or even close their doors, and stock markets around the world went into a nosedive.

Why? Because they misunderstood risk. They knew it was there, but they underestimated it. They thought it could never happen—surely someone else, probably a governmental entity or auditor, was watching. They thought they were too smart to be taken, figured that markets would always rise, looked to the left and to the right and saw other people proceeding on the same assumptions they held and thought that that many people could not possibly be wrong, thought that if they did not hop on this fast-moving train they would regret it and be considered a jerk by those who had gotten on board earlier.

Pick any of these mindsets you like, or consider some combination that seems plausible or likely in your experience. They can all be deadly. Sometimes we escape a misjudgment with little or no harm, but sometimes we do not, as the financial events of the past decade all too vividly indicate. Were this not enough, hundreds of other forms of corporate risk abound. This brief sampling provides some idea of the scope, frequency, and diversity of risk and the steps organizations take to counter it:

➤ Theft of intellectual property costs movie studios, recording companies, software producers, game manufacturers, and countless others billions of dollars each year.[3]

➤ Overseas business activity presents more exotic forms of risk.[4]

➤ The digital age brings with it its own forms of risk.[5]

➤ In times of economic downturn, crime may increase.[6]

➤ U.S. executives continue to be popular targets for kidnapping in a number of countries around the world. A report by IKV Pax Christi in Utrecht, Netherlands, cites 25,000 kidnappings of persons of all nationalities in 2006.[7]

➤ NanoGuardian, a division of NanoInk, a company that provides services designed to assist companies in brand protection by dealing with gray market and counterfeiting, announced the retention of a former executive assistant director of the FBI to serve on its security advisory board.[8]

➤ According to a report from the law firm of Gibson, Dunn & Crutcher LLP, U.S. authorities had filed Foreign Corrupt Practices Act (FCPA) cases against sixteen U.S. companies and their employees for illegal payments ("bribes") to foreign officials to secure business by the middle of 2008. This was a 78 percent increase from the same time the previous year.[9]

➤ A young man was apprehended by authorities in the middle of "an audacious plan to rule the black market in stolen credit cards."[10]

➤ A report indicates that a perhaps significant percentage of hospital-induced medical issues stem from the simple fact that medical personnel do not wash or change their "scrubs" (or hospital work clothing) often enough. A report on practices at the University of Maryland indicated that 65 percent of medical personnel change their lab coats less than once a week, and 15 percent change them less than once a month.[11]

➢ Interestingly, one of the longest-standing, most-respected, and heretofore invulnerable positions in corporations—the general counsel—is now subject to greatly increased levels of risk. In an article under the ominous heading "Corporate Crime," one writer makes the following statement with regard to corporate counsel and the environment in which they now find themselves: "Increasingly, the unwary or faint of heart find themselves behind bars."[12]

➢ Identify theft is now part of our common lexicon. Almost unknown a scant twenty years ago, the term and the activity it connotes are now accepted as a normal part of our daily existence.[13]

➢ Health care now consumes a significant part of our annual spending. The Centers for Medicare and Medicaid Services note that in 1965, U.S. health care consumers spent $42 billion. By 1991, that number had grown to $738 billion, an increase of 1,657 percent. By 1994, health care spending had climbed to $1.6 trillion, and spending in 2010 is estimated to exceed $2 trillion. How much of that money is lost to fraud or spent wastefully? Experts believe about 25 percent.[14]

➢ A Homeland Security Threat Assessment for 2008–2013 reports that continued instability in the Middle East and Africa, challenges in maintaining border security, and increasingly sophisticated cyberattacks are likely to pose security threats to the United States in coming years. At the same time, chemical, biological, radiological, and nuclear threats remain the most serious potential risks faced by the country.[15]

➢ Corporate executives, once pillars of their industries, fall with hard landings.[16]

➤ The Internet, which provides so much information, interconnectedness, and entertainment, poses its own threats.[17]

➤ Apparent corporate miscalculations also have the capability of presenting substantial risk in the form of financial losses.[18]

➤ In view of the spate of corporate failures and, as in the Madoff matter, outright fraud that attended the financial crisis of 2008–2009, the U.S. Department of Justice announced that it will, with substantial investigative assistance from the FBI, put a new focus on corporate fraud investigations. Indeed, press reports note that Congress has introduced two bills to fund the hiring of more FBI agents to address the issue.[19]

The list could go on for another hundred pages, but I hope the point has been made. Corporations and their employees face an enormous number and a wide variety of risks. This brings us to two essential points: how does an organization sense risk in its environment, and what does it do once risk is discovered?

NATURE AND RISK

In some ways, animals seem to understand the risk equation better than humans do. My wife and I live in a nature preserve in North Carolina and often enjoy watching the antics of the wildlife indigenous to the area. I have often seen squirrels foraging on the ground for bird seed that has fallen from the bird feeder above. As I observed them, I began to see a pattern. They would scamper around the feeder, find a seed, and then sit up on their haunches, scanning to the left and right. After the seed was consumed, they would scan again and then return to their search. Each cycle took about seven

seconds—seven foraging about and seven looking around. It occurred to me what they were doing. As small mammals, squirrels
have a number of predators—carnivores on the ground and raptors
in the air. Thus, even in the midst of something as necessary and
pleasurable as feeding, they devoted about half their time to scanning their environment for risk. Perhaps we can learn some valuable
lessons from our animal friends.

One is tempted to dismiss the squirrels as "dumb animals," not
worthy of our attention or of serious consideration when we think
about risk. But, I suggest we pause for a moment and look around at
the wreckage of quasi-governmental agencies and "name" Wall Street
firms that had internal and external audits, boards of directors, audit
committees, governmental oversight from regulatory bodies, and constant attention from the bright financial analysts who study and rate
such ventures. If all our checks and balances were so good, why did
so many institutions fail or require bailouts? Perhaps we should study
the squirrels more closely. Perhaps we should begin to rethink our
assumptions. I am not suggesting that corporations adopt the practices of squirrels and spend half their time scanning for risk, but (unless I have been called in to help handle problems at some very
atypical corporations) I believe that risk rarely consumes more than 1
percent of corporate revenue, if that. There is a big difference between
1 percent and 50 percent, so maybe the "dumb squirrels" aren't so
dumb, after all. And, when you think about it and look back at the
Top Fifty on any corporate ranking list of twenty or thirty years ago,
it is clear that a fair number of really "smart" corporations have disappeared. The February 2009 edition of *CFO* magazine ran a short article about companies that were delisted from the New York Stock
Exchange (NYSE) in 2008. The list is impressive and includes:

- ➤ R. H. Donnelley
- ➤ Spectrum Brands

> Tribune Company
> Pilgrim's Pride
> Downey Financial
> Idearc
> BearingPoint
> ML Macadamia Orchards
> VeraSun Energy
> Gottschalks
> GateHouse Media
> WCI Communications
> Feldman Mall Properties
> SunTimes Media Group
> Fremont General Corporation
> Scottish Re Group[20]

There is risk out there, and there are consequences when it is misjudged or mishandled.

THE BERNARD MADOFF SWINDLE

Let us turn to the Madoff matter and dissect it a bit more closely to see what went wrong. The apparent victims in this saga were not naive little old ladies in white gloves and flouncy hats, such as those depicted in the entertaining play and movie *The Producers*. These were the pros, the well heeled, the ones "in the know."

The scheme Madoff ran is almost a century old. It is called a "Ponzi" scheme, after the man who most famously ran one. The technique is simple—old investors are paid off with money from new investors, although there is little or no economic substance to the purported "investment." Madoff appears to have claimed to have a "secret" formula to make money, when in fact all he was doing was bringing in new money to replace "old" money."

According to press reports, even senior executives of the old and well-respected broker/dealer and investment firm Merrill Lynch were among Madoff's victims.[21] As more information becomes available, it seems individuals were not the only ones caught up in Madoff's scheme. Well-respected financial institutions also were drawn into the probable quagmire.[22] The saga seems to have a new chapter each day. A report by Fox News indicates that authorities have released the names of 13,000 Madoff customers/victims; a brief examination reveals the names of a Hall of Fame athlete, a major Hollywood actor, and one of the most prominent and probing talk show hosts on television.[23] A report by *The Wall Street Journal* revealed even more detail, suggesting that it appears that prominent personages such as director Steven Spielberg, producer Jeffrey Katzenberg, former Miss America Phyllis George, Hall of Fame pitcher Sandy Koufax, and famous actor John Malkovich could be among the lengthy roster of Madoff victims.[24]

The list, corporate or personal, could go on indefinitely, but the premise remains steady—failure to understand risk can lead to severe consequences. Apparently, social prominence, intellectual achievement, corporate size, and name recognition count for little when a faulty risk assumption has been made.

RISK—PROS AND CONS

While many struggle with risk, others prosper. A news account reports that the businesses of cobblers and automobile mechanics are booming, as the once prosperous repair their shoes rather than buy new ones and repair their cars instead of going shopping for a replacement.[25] So, too, with colleges and universities that have on-line learning courses. They are seeing a significant uptick in interest among those now concerned about how to better manage their distressed finances.[26] Strong, well-positioned companies are benefiting from the "thawing" credit markets. *The Wall Street Journal* reported early in 2009 that Cisco was selling $4 billion in bonds to not only reduce preexisting debt but also to stock its war chest for potential future acquisitions.[27]

While this book is exclusively about corporate risk, it may be instructive to spend a moment thinking about personal risk and how we deal with it. Indeed, we deal with it so often, in so many "small" ways, that we come to ignore it and assume it is just "natural."

Think, if you will, of a typical morning for a typical person. You live in a house and have a job. Your typical morning may well go something like this:

➤ You have an important meeting at the office at 9:00 A.M., and the office is about a thirty-minute commute. You want to be on time, allow for the possibility of bad traffic, and also build in some time to go over your materials before the meeting. Accordingly, you set the alarm for 7:00 A.M.

➤ When the alarm goes off, you put your hand lightly on the handrail and go downstairs, put the coffee on, let the dog out, and return to the bathroom to shower and get ready for the day. You perhaps have laid your clothes out the night before, to save time in the morning. You put the coffee on so that two things can be happening at once

➤ When you get back downstairs, you flick on the TV to see what is going on in the news, grab the newspaper from the front porch, and fix your breakfast of fruit, yogurt, and bran cereal.

> As you eat, you scan both the newspaper and the television to see what is going on in the world.

> You yell upstairs to the kids to get them up and moving to go to school. (Let's assume they're old enough to get themselves up, dressed, and out on their own.)

> You tuck the newspaper under your arm, grab your briefcase or computer bag, close the door behind you until it clicks, and get in the car. You fasten your seatbelt, again throw the news on the radio, check the rearview mirror to make sure the kids haven't left their bikes in the driveway, and back out of your garage.

> On the way to work you stop for stop signs and red lights and make sure traffic is clear before you enter an intersection. Within reason, you drive fairly close to the speed limit.

> On the way to the office you may use the time to check for voicemails or e-mails that came in overnight.

> When you get to the office, you park, hit the remote button to lock your car, enter the building, wave your identification card at the security guard, and enter the elevator, where you once again ignore the small card in a frame on the elevator wall.

> As you enter your office, you stop to check with your administrative assistant to see if anything is going on and to determine what progress he has made on a project you gave him yesterday.

Typical day, yes? About 90 percent of what happened in this example involved some effort to mitigate risk, but we do these things so often we no longer even think about them.

We use alarm clocks to make sure we are on time for business events. We tend to our personal hygiene and dress both for reasons of physical well-being and also for social and professional acceptability. We lightly touch the handrail on the stairs as a safeguard against falling. (Most building codes require a handrail for any flight of stairs four steps or greater. Thus, risk is codified for us, much like annual audits.) We let the dog out lest he befoul the carpet. We scan the news to see if there are developments—local, national, or international—that may affect us. We eat certain foods to try to maintain good health. We get the kids up so they will attend school and, we hope, do well. We close the door until it clicks to minimize the possibility of burglary, or worse. We use seat belts and check rearview mirrors to avoid accidents and the consequences thereof. We obey, usually, traffic regulations, to avoid accidents and to allow for the actions of those not as conscientious as we. We lock our vehicle to avoid theft, and we recognize the need for a security guard since we do not want people wandering into our work space for unknown reasons. We ignore the certificate in the elevator, which explains the last time the cab passed a safety examination. We talk to our administrative assistant to see if there is anything going on that we should be aware of and also to see if an important work project is going to get done on time.

Each and every one of those acts is a form of risk awareness (scanning our environment) or risk mitigation (taking actions to limit risk), but we do them so often, so routinely, and so naturally that we no longer even think about them. When we switch to the corporate world, however, risk issues often seem strange and burdensome. Certainly, some actions have become ingrained in normal routine, but it often seems that we tend to be less risk-aware in our corporate lives than in our personal sphere. Therein lies the danger.

We can never eliminate all risk; we can only manage it more effectively (a point made by Trent Gazzaway of Grant Thornton LLP in Chapter 3). A case that occurred close to my home in North

Carolina may be instructive. A young single man in his twenties had recently accepted a new job, and he moved to an apartment complex only several miles away. It was summertime, and he was lounging in a chair by the pool, when a sudden gust of wind came up. The burst of wind lifted an umbrella out of the bracket in which it sat, shading a poolside table. With the force of the wind behind it and its metal tip acting like the point of a spear, it struck the young man in the head. He died in the hospital a day or two later.

We cannot eliminate risk; we can only manage it, using the best information available and taking prudent steps to address it.

The movie *Catch Me If You Can* and the book that preceded it made Frank Abagnale something of a household name. The movie focuses on his life as an imposter, but it was his primary work as a forger that led him into that double life. Since the time of his misdeeds, he has spent many years as a consultant to financial institutions and law enforcement, including much work with the FBI. His website carries an interesting observation from one who obviously knows more than most about the subject: Abagnale notes that "punishment for fraud and recovery of funds are so rare, prevention is the only viable course of action."[28]

NOTES

1. Kurt F. Reding et al., *Internal Auditing: Assurance and Consulting Services* (Altamonte Springs, Fla.: Institute of Internal Auditors Research Foundation, 2007), pp. 1–4.
2. John A. Rohr, "Ethics in Public Administration: A State-of-the-Discipline Report," in *Public Administration: The State of the Discipline*, eds. Naomi B. Lynn and Aaron Wildavsky (Chatham, N.J.: Chatham House, 1990), p. 97.
3. Brian Stelter and Brad Stone, "Digital Pirates Winning Battle with Major Hollywood Studios," *New York Times*, February 5, 2009, p. A-1.
4. "Justifiable Risk?" *Merger & Acquisition Focus*, Everingham & Kerr, Inc., Laurel, N.J. (October–November 2008), p. 5.

5. Bill Coffin, "Holding the Line against Cyber Liability," *Wall Street Journal*, September 24, 2008, p. A-17.

6. Bill Zalud and Terry Maddry, "Does a Bad Economy Spur Higher Crime?" *Security* Magazine (November 2008), p. 14.

7. Nathan Vardi, "Kidnap Inc.," *Forbes* (October 13, 2008), p. 94.

8. Pharmalive.com, "Distinguished FBI and Pharmaceutical Security Expert to Lead in NanoGuardian Advisory Board," press release, January 19, 2009.

9. "Gunning for Global Graft," *CFO* Magazine (September 2008), p. 19.

10. Kevin Poulsen, "Catch Me If You Can," *Wired* Magazine (January 2009).

11. Betsy McCaughey, "Hospital Scrubs Are a Dirty, Germy Mess," *Wall Street Journal*, January 8, 2009, p. A-13.

12. Steven Andersen, "The Hot Seat: Increasingly, Criminal Liability Passes to the General Counsel," *Inside Counsel* Magazine (October 2008), p. 38.

13. "Special Report: Threat of Identity Theft on the Rise in Wake of Global Financial Crisis" (advertisement), *Wall Street Journal*, January 8, 2009, p. B-3.

14. Rebecca S. Busch, *Healthcare Fraud: Auditing and Detection Guide* (Hoboken, N.J.: Wiley, 2008), p. 1.

15. "DHS Forecasts Top Security Threats for the Next Five Years," *Security Director News* (February 2009), p. 2.

16. Amir Efrati, "Ex-AIG Executive Is Sentenced to Four Years," *Wall Street Journal*, January 28, 2009, p. C-3.

17. William M. Bulkeley, "Suit Alleges Internet Espionage," *Wall Street Journal*, February 2, 2009, p. C-2.

18. Scott Patterson and Amir Ng, "Deutsch Bank Fallen Leader Left Behind $1.8 Billion Hole," *Wall Street Journal*, February 6, 2009, p. A-1.

19. Carrie Johnson, "Justice Department Putting New Focus on Combating Corporate Fraud," *Washington Post*, February 12, 2009, p. A-6.

20. "Companies Suspended from Trading on the NYSE in 2008," *CFO* Magazine (February 2009), p. 14.

21. Randall Smith, "Ex-Merrill Executives Got Burned by Madoff," *Wall Street Journal*, January 30, 2009, p. C-1.

22. Jenny Strausburg, "Mass Mutual Burned by Madoff," *Wall Street Journal*, December 22, 2008, p. C-1.

23. Fox Television News, February 5, 2009.

24. Dionne Searcey and Amir Efrati, "Madoff Clients Exposed," *Wall Street Journal*, February 6, 2009, p. A-1.

25. Sarah E. Needleman, "In Sole Revival, the Recession Gives Beleaguered Cobblers New Traction," *Wall Street Journal*, February 2, 2009, p. A-1.

26. Alina Dizik, "A Boost in Online Money Courses," *Wall Street Journal*, February 4, 2009, p. D-3.

27. Ben Worthen, and Kellie Geressy, "Bond Market in Winter Thaw: Cisco Seizes Opening to Raise $4 Billion; Credit Easing for Best-Rated Firms," *Wall Street Journal*, February 10, 2009, p. A-1.

28. Website, Frank W. Abagnale, February 16, 2009.

2.

· ·

FRAUD AS AN EXAMPLE OF RISK

· · · · · · · · · · · · · · · ·

As has been noted, risk comes in a wide variety of forms. I have dealt with a fair amount of it, as have my friends and colleagues who have been kind enough to share their thoughts, observations, and experiences. In this chapter I discuss fraud, specifically occupational fraud, the subject on which I have spent the majority of my professional time in the private sector. Occupational fraud is, in and of itself, a significant risk for any corporation, but it is also instructive, since its causation and many of its characteristics often apply to corporate risk in general.

There are only three means by which one human being can take money or something of value from another. The first is force, or threat of force, and this is called armed robbery, mugging, carjacking, or extortion. The second is stealth, and this is seen in auto theft, shoplifting, and burglary. The third is by far the most pernicious, for it not only results in the loss of things of value but also inflicts sometimes deep psychological injury as well. It is called betrayal of trust.

All frauds are an abuse of trust, whether it is trust in a family member or friend, a business associate, or a corporate entity or institution.

Fraud is defined in Black's Law Dictionary as follows:

All multifarious means which human ingenuity can devise, and which are resorted to by one individual to get an advantage over another by false suggestions or suppression of truth. It includes all surprise, trick, cunning, or dissembling, and any unfair way which another is cheated.[1]

This definition covers pretty much all fraud, but occupational fraud presents a special risk, for it is the act of an employee stealing from his employer. Thus, the fox that raids the chicken coop does not come from outside; it is already inside, where it is known, accepted, trusted, and familiar with where to locate the chickens while minimizing its chance of detection.

A true visionary and stalwart leader in the field of fraud, Joe Wells, defines occupational fraud as follows: "The use of one's occupation for personal enrichment through the deliberate misuse or misapplication of the employing organization's resource or assets."[2]

ASSOCIATION OF CERTIFIED FRAUD EXAMINERS

In discussing fraud in general and occupational fraud in particular, I rely heavily on the work and research of the Association of Certified Fraud Examiners (ACFE). Based in Austin, Texas, this organization was started in 1989 by former FBI special agent Joe Wells and two close associates, Jim Ratley, a former Dallas police officer, and Kathie Green. After leaving the FBI, Joe had worked as a forensic consultant, dealing largely with both personal and corporate fraud issues. Over time, he came to realize that the field, such as it was, would benefit from increased training based upon an organized body of knowledge. Thus was ACFE created. The organization shortly thereafter created a certificate—Certified Fraud Examiner (CFE)—for those who met educational and work experience require ments and passed a rigorous examination. Today, the CFE designation is recognized throughout the private and professional sectors and also by governmental agencies such as the U.S. Postal Inspection Service, the Federal Bureau of Investigation, and the General Accounting Office. By 2009, just twenty years after its founding, ACFE had almost 50,000 members in more than 120 countries. Over the years, Wells has been recognized numerous times by professional bodies for his foresight and pioneering work.

ACFE ANNUAL REPORT ON FRAUD

One of the great services ACFE provides, in addition to its many other good works, is to publish an annual report, *Report to the Nation* (*RTN*). This report, which is available free of charge on ACFE's website, annually captures the experiences of more than 1,000 CFEs who have volunteered to provide detailed and specific information on the cases they have worked on during the previous year. Many members are internal auditors in corporations and other institutions; they provide a rare view of the type and frequency of fraud risk faced by such entities. Still other members are independent CPAs, members of professional services firms that perform forensic work on behalf of clients, law enforcement officials, educators, and students.

As of this writing, the most recent edition of *RTN* covers 2009, but the data it provides about fraud incidents and those who perpetrate them have remained remarkably consistent over the years and serve to help us better understand the nature of fraud risk and therefore risk in general. That this is so speaks to the nature of risk itself. All fraud is committed by people. There are no naturally occurring frauds. So, too, with much risk. Some of it is random (e.g., floods, hurricanes), but the majority of it stems from human actions, intended or inadvertent. Thus, ACFE's reporting provides insight and value.

In considering the *RTN* data, it is important to note what the report does not capture. It does not capture or attempt to capture the minor acts of dishonesty that occur every day in almost every organization—taking pens and pencils home, making personal calls on the company telephone and on company time, using the office computer to surf the Web or send jokes and videos to friends (or receive them). The findings listed here concern only significant, purposeful fraud:

- ➤ Occupational fraud in the United States costs companies and organizations almost $1 trillion each year.
- ➤ The average corporation loses 5–6 percent of revenue each year to occupational fraud.
- ➤ Roughly half the offenders are male, and half are female.
- ➤ Most offenders are between forty-five and fifty-five years of age.
- ➤ Well over 90 percent have no criminal history of fraud.
- ➤ Most offenders have been with the organization for an average of ten to fifteen years.
- ➤ Fraud is scalable; the amount of the fraud loss is proportional to organizational position. Thus, assuming people at

various levels go bad, there is a ratio that has held up well over the years. If a line employee steals a dollar, a manager will steal four dollars, and an executive will steal sixteen.

➤ The average fraud lasts eighteen months, and the vast majority of them increase with time.

➤ Traditional controls, such as internal and external audits, are not particularly effective at uncovering occupational fraud. Most frauds are discovered by accident or because of a tip.

➤ Having an effective hotline in the organization reduces fraud losses by about 50 percent. A hotline does not reduce the incidence of fraud; roughly the same number of frauds will occur. Hotlines do reduce the duration and, thereby, the amount of the loss. (Note the CERT-USSS study cited later in this chapter regarding the surprising number of people who are aware of, even if they are not involved in, fraud incidents.)

➤ Organizations rarely refer frauds for prosecution; indeed, there is no central collection point for data concerning such events.

➤ Insurance coverage rarely replaces more than 25 percent of the loss, and often it replaces none.

While these figures are sobering, they must be viewed objectively. First, although all data come from CFEs, they reflect self-reporting. Academic researchers tend to be leery of self-reporting, since there may be a tendency to either report inaccurately or to exaggerate the magnitude of the issues one grapples with in the course of one's work. Second, the methodology used by ACFE is to take the percentage lost to fraud (5–6 percent of organizational revenue, again an estimate provided by the reporting CFEs) and apply it against the gross domestic product of the United States for a given reporting year. This is where the figure of almost $1 trillion comes from. Again, academic researchers would have issues with this methodology.

In the great scheme of things, however, these are somewhat minor quibbles, for the ACFE data are the best—indeed, the only—data we have on this issue. And the ACFE data have an inherent advantage. Since the CFEs reporting are usually internal auditors and investigators within the victim company, they have access to personnel files. Thus, they know the age, educational level, sex, length of tenure, organizational position, and so on of the person who committed the fraud. These data are usually unavailable when a fraud is perpetrated by an outsider. Accordingly, we should be thankful for the insight ACFE has given us into the world of occupational fraud.

We must accept that occupational fraud is a form of organizational risk and, perhaps, a fairly significant one, but what does this say about risk in general? It suggests that, while we tend to focus on external risk (bad people doing bad things), a fair amount of risk walks through the front door every morning wearing an employee ID badge. These need not be people intent on stealing, as are those who commit occupational fraud, but they may present quite serious risk nonetheless. The employee who is lazy, indifferent, dissatisfied, vengeful, or simply overworked can greatly increase organizational risk by not doing their jobs, reporting data late, reporting inaccurate data, and failing to perform necessary assurance duties, from making certain a food-processing machine is thoroughly cleaned to ensuring that a valve is fully closed.

When dealing with risk, we must look both outside and inside. Inside is often overlooked, or at least minimized as secondary to outside threat. This can be a massive mistake. It usually is made for one of two reasons. Since we, or our organization, have already made a decision to hire certain people, we simply assume that they are both trustworthy and conscientious. To assume otherwise is to question our own initial judgment, and this is not an easy thing to do.

Second, suspicion, much less confrontation, is not easy. However, it is much easier to accomplish with strangers (those outside the organization, whatever their relationship to it) than with insiders, those who are "our own." Accordingly, it is often avoided, sometimes with tragic consequences.

The travails of a client I once had may help illustrate these points. It was a company that manufactured the sort of equipment used in pools—underwater lights, ladders, diving boards, cleaning equipment, and the like. The company had recently purchased a company in a similar line of business in a distant state. As with many such acquisitions, it struggled to integrate internal control systems of various sorts. Thus, managers had a poor or incomplete understanding of the acquired company's "financials."

After several months, they observed a disturbing trend. Sales were up, but profits were down. Unlike many clients, they quickly concluded that they were the victim of a fraud of some sort. They hired one organization that, after completing an exhaustive analysis, concluded that there was no fraud to be found. The analysis, while detailed, failed to produce an answer to the issue of falling profits. Thus, the company I worked for at the time was brought in to take a second look at the problem. We found it fairly quickly.

When the client purchased the other company, it failed to realize an important point: the company had outsourced its inventory management to an outside vendor. This vendor handled the company's supply of the raw materials and parts it used in making its products. However, there was a clause in the contract that management had failed to appreciate. The company handling the inventory was paid a percentage of the amount it ordered, and there was a 10 percent variance in how much it ordered (that is, it could order 10 percent more or less than was needed.)

How did the subcontractor proceed? Of course, it tended to overorder, since this increased its profits on the contract. Thus did the acquiring company, our client, incur high carrying costs for inventory not needed. The more it produced, the more money it lost.

Of course, this is not the result of fraud; it is a classic case of suffering from not knowing what is going on. It happens more often than you might suspect.

COMPUTER EVIDENCE RESPONSE TEAM

A number of studies done by the Computer Evidence Response Team (CERT) at Carnegie-Mellon University and the U.S. Secret Service (USSS) highlight this issue, but perhaps none so powerfully as a study jointly performed and released by the two organizations working together (CERT-USSS) in August 2004. (All materials and studies are available at the CERT website.)

The study, titled "Insider Threat Study: Illicit Cyber Activity in the Banking and Finance Sector," is interesting not only in its own right but also because many of its findings correlate so closely with the data accumulated by ACFE over a ten-year period.

The CERT-USSS study looked at insider incidents in the banking and financial industry during the period 1996–2002. A total of twenty-three incidents, committed by twenty-six insiders, were studied. Fifteen involved fraud, four involved theft of intellectual property (IP), and four were attempts to sabotage information systems or networks. These findings provide us with a better idea of the range, nature, and methodology of insider threats:

> In about 70 percent of the incidents, perpetrators "employed simple, legitimate user commands."
> In 70 percent of the incidents, perpetrators "exploited or attempted to exploit systemic vulnerabilities in applications and/or processes or procedures."
> 78 percent of the perpetrators were authorized users.
> In 43 percent of the incidents, perpetrators used their own name or password.
> Only 26 percent of the time did the perpetrator use someone else's computer or password.
> Only 23 percent of the perpetrators held technical positions that gave them special knowledge of computer systems.
> Only 17 percent of the perpetrators held system administrator positions that gave them extraordinary computer system access.
> 87 percent of the incidents were planned in advance.
> Amazingly, in 85 percent of the incidents, others knew of the activity.
> In 31 percent of the incidents, the planning behavior was noticed by others.
> 65 percent of the time, the perpetrators, interestingly, did not consider the consequences of their actions.
> 81 percent of the time, the objective was financial gain (note that theft of intellectual property can produce substantial financial gain, depending upon how the material is used).
> In 23 percent of the incidents, revenge was the primary motivation.
> In 15 percent of the incidents, dissatisfaction with the employer was the primary driver.
> In another 15 percent, the desire for respect was a motivating factor. (The movie *Breach* was based on a true incident

involving an FBI agent turned Russian spy, who believed, among other things, that he was underappreciated for his skills and insight.)

> The perpetrators ranged in age from eighteen to fifty-nine years, and 42 percent were female.

> 54 percent were single, and 31 percent were married.

> Only 15 percent were, prior to the incident, considered difficult to manage, and only 4 percent were considered untrustworthy.[3]

Ironically, it now appears that Carnegie-Mellon University may itself have been the victim of a massive fraud that could cost it $49 million, the amount it invested with two hedge fund operators, Paul Greenwood and Stephen Walsh. The two men were arrested early in 2009 by the FBI and are suspected of perhaps squandering at least $553 million of client funds on lavish lifestyles that included mansions, $100,000 show ponies, and $80,000 collectible teddy bears. It thus appears that even those who study risk are themselves susceptible to it.[4]

What the CERT-USSS study tells us is somewhat frightening. Those within our corporate environments who may, for whatever reason(s), create a significant risk incident look pretty much like everyone else. There are no obvious signs by which to identify them as different or that make them stand out from the general employee population. Therefore, we tend to ignore them, assuming that if they have a company badge they are "OK," and focus our threat awareness outward.

While external threats are a serious issue, we have a false sense of security if we believe no risk comes from inside.

This view is confirmed by a recent study reported in *The Wall Street Journal*, which indicates that there has been a recent increase in internal corporate crimes, often by "the most trusted workers." The story goes on to note a study released in November 2008 by the Institute for Corporate Productivity in conjunction with HR.com that revealed that 20 percent of employees polled said workplace theft has become a moderate to very big issue in recent years. It also mentions a survey by Jack L. Haynes Inc. of twenty-four large retailers employing more than 2.3 million people. The survey indicated that one in twenty-eight workers was apprehended for stealing in 2007.[5] And, we must remember, these are only the ones who got caught.

WHY DO THEY DO IT?

One is tempted to ask the obvious question: "If we cannot trust our own people, whom can we trust?"

A possible answer may come from a noted educator, theorist, and writer who has labored for many years trying to answer this and other, related questions. His name is Dr. Steve Albrecht, and his comments are insightful:

> Fraud occurs when pressure, opportunity and rationalization come together. Most people have pressures. Everyone rationalizes. When internal controls are absent or overridden, everyone . . . has an opportunity.[6]

Let us return to the CERT-USSS study. Please check the statistics I presented. How many people acted out of revenge, how many acted because of dissatisfaction with the company, how many acted without thinking of the consequences? "Rationalization" can be a powerful incentive that can blind the otherwise intelligent to the consequences of their actions. While we have considered fraud as an example, these very same human motivations can impact almost any form of organizational risk.

Much interesting research has been published by a noted psychologist, Michael J. Apter, who has closely studied the various mechanisms and behaviors that some (perhaps more than we realize) of us utilize to seek risk and excitement, even if it involves "breaking the rules."[7]

As the statistics presented earlier in this chapter show, those who commit occupational fraud pretty much look like us. Why do they do it?

Thus far, there has been little more than informed speculation regarding the answer to this question. I have discussed these issues not only with my esteemed colleagues but also with the many students—mainly midcareer professionals in auditing, accounting, teaching, finance, or law—whom I have taught over the past fifteen years. They come back with a number of possible motivations:

➢ Midlife crisis; wants to have a little fun.

➢ Has a new love interest and needs the money to support it.

➢ Has a gambling or drug addiction.

➢ Thinks a lot of other people are doing it, so she might as well also.

➢ Thinks that the big guys get away with it, why shouldn't I get a piece of the action?

➢ Thinks he is smart and can beat the system.

➢ Needs the money to pay college tuition, mortgage, medical bills, or other expenses.

➢ Believe it is only a "loan" that can be paid back.

➢ Want to get "even" with the company since he did not get the bonus/promotion he thinks he deserved.

> Has a clean record, so believes she will face no heavy penalty even if she gets caught.

> Thinks he needs to protect himself since the company is downsizing and the industry is weak.

> Thinks that the company is so stupid and poorly run that it deserves to be taken advantage of.

> If nobody knows, who cares? (No harm, no foul.)

> Suggests that since the company has been ripping customers off for years, it's only fair to rip it off just a little.

> Believes she is going to take only a little bit and the company can afford it; it will, however, be enough to move/start her own business/get out of debt.

It is, unfortunately, my duty to advise you of a fact both surprising and sad—we know more about serial killers than we do about those who commit crimes against their employers and investors. We are beginning to study this issue (I am on one such study team), but we have a long way to go.

Those who commit fraud are not "bad" people, in the normal sense. They are not gang members; they do not carry guns or knives or display abundant tattoos; they are not uneducated; and they do not have long criminal records. In short, they are the "soccer moms and dads" who look very much like us in every way, but one day they go bad. The essential question remains: why?

I have interviewed such people often in their offices and cubicles. They have the normal adornments of middle-class existence—photos of children and pets, awards from their company or other organizations with which they may be involved, small bowls of candy. Normal in every way, except that they chose, on a given day, to steal.

Why do they do it? We do not know, although researchers are

beginning to develop theories. With effort, we may someday develop more understanding.

Not only are corporations prone to such risks, but we as individuals are, as well, in both our corporate and our private lives. An article in *The Wall Street Journal* by Stephen Greenspan, professor emeritus of educational psychology at the University of Connecticut, suggests several theories offered to explain such tendencies. Himself a self-described victim of the Madoff swindle, Greenspan notes that such gullibility is hardly new. He mentions Charles Mackey's nineteenth-century book, *Extraordinary Popular Delusion and the Madness of Crowds*, in which Mackey discusses, among other things, the "tulip mania" that had swept Holland centuries earlier, inducing wealthy people to trade their houses for several tulip bulbs.

In our own time, Greenspan notes the pronouncements, in 1996, of then–Federal Reserve chairman Alan Greenspan (no relation) about the "irrational exuberance" he believed to be sweeping financial markets. Professor Greenspan observes that this, in his opinion, is reflective of the "feedback loop" phenomenon, in which investors are swayed by nothing more than the actions and apparent success of other investors.[8]

The Institute for Fraud Prevention (IFP) is a group that has been formed to begin to try to answer questions about fraud and those who commit it. The idea for IFP came from the legendary Joe Wells, founder of the Association of Certified Fraud Examiners, and, although it took a few years to get up and running, it is now in full operation. Funded by corporate contributions and currently administered by West Virginia University, its purpose, among others, is to encourage and fund multidisciplinary research in the causation of fraud. It is an interesting subject, for as threatening as it is, fraud has been little studied in the academic and research literature. Indeed, many of the most useful theories that attempt to "explain" it go back decades.

If IFP is successful in its quest and mission, not only will the field of fraud prevention, detection, and investigation benefit, but so will all professionals and disciplines concerned with organizational risk. Fraud is, after all, only another form of organizational risk.

NOTES

1. Henry Campbell Black, *Black's Law Dictionary*, 5th ed. (St. Paul, Minn.: West, 1979), p. 468.
2. Joseph T. Wells, *Occupational Fraud and Abuse* (Austin, Tex.: Obsidian, 1997), p. 3.
3. Computer Evidence Response Team and U.S. Secret Service, *Insider Threat Study: Illicit Cyber Activity in the Banking and Finance Sector* (Pittsburgh: CERT, 2004).
4. Steve Stecklow, Chad Bray, and Jenny Strausburg, "Pair Lived Large on Fraud, U.S. Says," *Wall Street Journal*, February 26, 2009, p. A-1.
5. Sarah E. Needleman, "Businesses Say Theft by Their Workers Is Up," *Wall Street Journal*, December 11, 2008, p. B-8.
6. W. Steve Albrecht, "Employee Fraud," *Internal Auditor* (October 1996), p. 28.
7. Michael J. Apter, *Danger: Our Quest for Excitement* (Oxford: Oneworld, 2007).
8. Stephen Greenspan, "Why We Keep Falling for Financial Scams," *Wall Street Journal*, January 3–4, 2009, p. W-1.

3.

. . . .

FRONTLINE INTERVIEWS WITH RISK MANAGEMENT EXPERTS

. . . .

As noted in the Acknowledgments section, in writing this book, I have benefited greatly from the kind and generous assistance of many friends and professional colleagues. In this chapter, I present their stories, their thoughts, and their insights. I wrote the words, but they reviewed, corrected, amended, expanded, and corrected them. These are folks who have been on the front lines of risk management and have learned much through their experiences. I include these "first-person" accounts not for the sake of "telling war stories" but to establish the basis for a more detailed discussion of the various issues and quandaries they raise in the chapters that follow. We will refer to their stories, wisdom, and insights often as we proceed through the rest of this book. My colleagues were dealing with real situations, not textbook simulations. They, along with their organizations and clients, had risk that was real, immediate, and substantial.

They have "been there and done that," and they have learned from their experiences. I think we all can, as well.

Throughout this book, I present other, more specific interviews, but these are so broadly based and comprehensive that they are most instructive when they stand alone.

HENRY RISTUCCIA

Henry Ristuccia, a twenty-year veteran of the Big Four professional services firm Deloitte & Touche LLP (D&T), now heads the firm's Governance and Risk Management practice in Manhattan. A partner for twelve years, he previously headed the regional Computer Assurance Services practice (now called Enterprise Risk Services by D&T).

Henry was featured, along with one of his associates, in the February 2009 e-edition of *Directors and Boards* magazine, in which they set forth their thoughts on risk and on corporations' understanding of it and response to it.

A quick trip to the D&T website and an easy search for terms such as risk management and risk intelligence will produce a volume of information as to how D&T sees these issues and the services the firm offers to assist clients in dealing with them. One interesting approach, considering the current global economic downturn, is that these conditions highlight the fact that, as they put it, "something is broken." By that they mean that it appears that a range of corporations and institutions made some flawed decisions and assumptions regarding the type and amount of risk they faced.

D&T, like other firms, is a business, and to survive it must offer clients services of demonstrable value. D&T's approach has several facets. One is the concept of Integrated Market Offering (IMO) Accelerators. Simply put, these are tools to help a corporation or an industry better assess, understand, and plan for risk. These offerings seem to have found a warm reception, as the rating service Forrester recently named D&T the "pre-eminent risk consultant."

Among the many tools D&T offers is a nine-step process geared toward improving a corporation's risk "intelligence"—its ability to make informed decisions about risk and thereby to make more informed moves to deal with it. The process, in microcosm, proceeds as follows:

1. **Come to a common definition of risk.** Certainly, there is risk in every area of corporate operations, but some risks are greater than others, and some risks run laterally through various operational areas. These must be prioritized and used to build a manageable risk framework for the corporate entity.

2. **Develop a common risk framework**. If every element in the corporation runs off in a different direction in trying to anticipate, understand, assess, and deal with risk, much confusion and wasted energy may result.

3. **Define roles and responsibilities**. Once a risk profile has been identified and prioritized, Henry believes it is important to establish "who does what."

4. **Establish transparency for governing bodies.** A "governing body" may be the board of directors, the shareholders, institutional investors, or some other entity, but the objective of this step is to make the "risk plan" understandable to those who have a key interest and to those whose support may be required.

5. **Adopt a common risk infrastructure.** Various groups and associations, from the federal government to the Committee of Sponsor-

ing Organizations and beyond, have promulgated guidelines and standards with regard to risk. Many elements of these pronouncements overlap, but each set of guidelines is different in some way from the others. It behooves the organization to decide which set seems to best meet its needs.

6. **Clarify executive management responsibility.** Those at the top of the corporate structure must have a clear understanding of their roles and responsibilities; otherwise, conflicting and disjointed messages will be sent to those further down. When this happens, it is highly doubtful that a coherent risk management program will emerge.

7. **Use objective assurance monitoring.** Here the effort is to try to ensure that the framework and infrastructure used to monitor, assess, and define risk is consistent across corporate boundaries. There is a second and too-often overlooked piece here—information assurance. Risk assessment is only as good as the data upon which it is based. As I will note elsewhere in this book, I have seen too many corporate data systems that rely on poor, disorganized, out-of-date, or skewed data. Were one to base a key risk assessment on data suffering from one of these maladies, the assessment itself might be seriously flawed.

8. **Emphasize business unit responsibility.** This is the stage where the risk assessment and mitigation process gets down to the "nuts and bolts" level. Risk assessment and mitigation are, like the proverbial chain, only as strong as the weakest link. Clear and consistent guidance must be provided, because the risk model is only as strong as its foundation.

9. **Support pervasive functions.** Much risk data will come from main-line business functions, such as Information Technology (IT)

and Finance. These must be properly staffed with people who have the right skill sets and the right technology to perform at an optimum level.

A companion to D&T's nine-step model is what the firm has trademarked as its "Deep Dive" approach. This entails involving key personnel from all related areas to probe and understand the true risk environment. Thus, those from the shop floor may meet with mid-level and even senior managers to make sure that all pertinent information is shared and that folks at the top are proceeding on solid information and not relying on assumptions.

Henry Ristuccia has a number of other observations on risk in a corporate environment:

> **It is often unclear who "owns" risk, which may be a product of the fact that it is often seen as being "siloed."** There is marketing risk, production risk, environmental and safety risk, foreign exchange risk, and so on. While each entity may have risk sensing and mitigation mechanisms in place, these are rarely coordinated across functional lines and rarely achieve a maximal level of effectiveness in any consistent manner.

> **There is often confusion as to boundaries and meanings of terms much heard today: corporate governance, risk management (or mitigation), and corporate compliance.** While various texts define these terms in detail, even long-time professionals in the field note that there is still some confusion as to their meaning. This is not a deadly situation, since the terms are widely accepted and acknowledged in the corporate world. Indeed, they are closely interrelated. It may be useful to think of them as three views of the same object—the avoidance of risk.

➤ **In a world as broad and as diverse as "risk," everything cannot be a top priority.** Common sense and organizational resources so dictate. Thus, Henry favors a "desert island" approach, a concept he learned many years ago during a training program (there are variations of this approach, such as the NASA moon simulation game, which I used for many years in training programs). They all have the same objective. Imagine that you are stranded on a desert island or the lunar surface. You have twenty pieces of equipment available to you to assist in your survival, but you can carry only six. Which six do you pick? The game is normally played in a classroom setting, wherein everyone gets a list and makes his or her own decisions. Then, using the same scenario, the class breaks into groups of four or five and comes up with a group list. Invariably, the "group" decision comes closer to the list of logical decisions produced by the game's developers than does any individual more than 90 percent of the time. There are two lessons to be learned here with regard to risk: First, the more input you have, the better your decisions will probably be, and, second, given the dimensions of risk, you must prioritize, lest you be overwhelmed or try to do everything at once and wind up doing nothing too well.

➤ **Finally, there is the issue of what happens if your best efforts fail.** You have recognized risk, you have assessed it, prioritized it, and taken prudent steps to mitigate it. Generically, these are called "preventive controls"; you are trying to prevent bad things from happening. But, every now and then, even your best efforts are not enough. Your second line of defense is made up of detective controls. Do you have systems in place to ensure that if something does go wrong, you will at least learn about it before the problem becomes too large or too widespread? The pairing of these two systems vastly improves the corporation's ability to deal with risk.

Henry's comments are insightful, but also fairly common to those who work in the field of risk. We are somewhat like old detectives, who have seen so much of what we deal with that we begin to accept it as just part of the human condition. More jaded observers may call it a cynical view of the world, as if our exposure were somehow elemental, when indeed it is fundamental. We have simply spent too much time beating our heads against collective walls, and we have become dizzy from the exercise.

No one is perfect on risk, even those who deal with it often. But, we can become better. We cannot eliminate all risk, but we can become more adept at identifying and dealing with it, thus reducing our exposure to its consequences.

An example may be in order. Over the years I have noted a tendency in clients to try to quickly "compartmentalize" an issue at hand. I have heard the terms many times—"We had a bad apple"; "Let's put this behind us"; "Let's move on."

Such responses are understandable for a number of reasons. (I talk only about fraud, my primary field.) Dealing with ugly situations is painful. Trust has been betrayed. There is a sense of embarrassment at having been played for a fool. The entire process is uncomfortable and expensive. We have an incentive to move quickly past the issue at hand.

That is fine, but . . . we take such actions at the risk of creating yet more risk. Here is a case in point.

I once had a client who manufactured industrial equipment that was both complex and quite expensive. The company had eighty-five sales offices in North America and had begun to notice problems in the financial results reported by several sales offices. We were called in to analyze the situation and found that sales offices in three separate cities (top performers all) had misreported their financial numbers.

The client was, as you might suspect, horrified. It took immediate remedial action and was prepared to be done with the matters. As a matter of professional courtesy, we suggested the client might care to see if the problems were more widespread. Our premise was simple: If three of eighty-five offices had issues, could there also be issues in the remaining eighty-two?

The client reacted in horror, expecting such an effort to create huge cost. In response, we noted that we had abundant corporate data provided by the client stored in our forensic computer systems and that, understanding now how such schemes had been carried out, we could quickly and cheaply analyze the remaining sales offices. After due consideration, we were given permission to proceed, and the ensuing computer analysis indicated an additional twelve sales offices had problems. To the client's credit, it assembled an internal task force of its own people to address these issues.

It is useful to return to Henry's astute and experienced observations. Not every issue is fraud, but if we deal with but one issue at a time simply because that's the one that has come to our attention, we risk missing other forms of risk that lie dormant for the moment but that will eventually erupt.

TRENT GAZZAWAY

Trent Gazzaway understands risk. As managing partner of the Corporate Governance practice for Grant Thornton LLP, an international professional services firm, he deals with it every day. His career prepared him well for this task; he has conducted or supervised many audits, internal control valuations, and financial reporting investigations. He has seen what can go wrong and also understands how to move prudently to mitigate risk.

His professional achievements have led him to a leadership role in various risk-oriented organizations, among them the Open Compliance and Ethics Group and the Enterprise Risk Management Initiative at North Carolina State University's College of Management. He was appointed by the Committee of Sponsoring Organizations (COSO) of the Treadway Commission to lead a project to develop guidance regarding effective monitoring of internal controls in major organizations. He has, as one might suspect, been duly recognized for his work, having been named one of the "100 Most Influential People in Finance" twice by *Treasury & Risk Management* magazine and "Auditor of the Year" by the Institutional Investor's *Compliance Reporter* publication.

When asked to ruminate about his long experience dealing with risk and what he has seen and learned, Gazzaway offers the following insights:

➢ **Risk is not only a corporate function; it is part of management's job at every level.** Certainly, managers have other responsibilities, but they must achieve a balance between their task-oriented responsibilities and their role as managers and mitigators of risk. This is an important point, as Gazzaway counsels that the concept of risk is not only something to be avoided but, since it is inevitable, to be managed.

It is easy enough to appoint a chief risk officer, provide a staff, and be done with it. Gazzaway counsels that this can be too simple a "solution" for too important an issue. If risk is seen as someone else's job, then others need not worry about it, since the risk officer will call if there is an issue. Everyone, Gazzaway believes, must be involved in risk management. The key, again, is to find the proper balance between the pursuit of opportunity and the mitigation of risk.

➢ **The key element in the foundation of risk management is risk assessment.** Because it forms the basis from which all other risk management flows, it is vital that risk assessment be done properly, lest the organization proceed on a faulty premise or misunderstanding of its risk environment. To achieve this, Gazzaway advises, the organization must have "the right people around the table." By this he means that risk is not always the exclusive domain of the "C suite" executives with the nice offices. Organizations would be wise to involve key personnel from many levels, at least in an initial assessment of risk, to gain a better base-level understanding of their risk environment, since risk can come from many places and take in many forms.

➢ **An organization's approach to risk must be scaled.** To use the old phrase, "one size does not fit all," Gazzaway advises that many popular approaches, like Enterprise Risk Management (ERM), can be of great value, but they should not be applied in a "take it out of the box and slap it on" manner. The organization must review and select its risk management tools carefully and tailor them to the unique character, culture, and characteristics of the enterprise. If the risk assessment is done properly, he believes, the vast majority of all risk can be properly identified and addressed.

➢ **Risk is ubiquitous; not all of it can be foreseen.** We are bounded by the limits of human endurance and intellect. There are also the real-world constraints of time and money. Yet, if we approach risk mitigation prudently, we can identify and address the vast majority of threats. Gazzaway also recommends that smaller organizations not get caught up in the temptation to look like the big guys. An effective risk mitigation strategy for a smaller organization may be much less formal and structured than that of a major multinational, but it can still be effective if properly executed.

Although deeply involved in COSO and similar entities, Gazzaway believes there is still much to be done to improve corporations' management of risk. Certainly, he notes, COSO and other bodies have done vital work in establishing the guiding principles of risk mitigation and corporate governance, but implementation is still the key. He, and others, still labor to develop workable "domains" of guidance for organizations to guide them on how to best achieve implementation. The principles are "science," but their implementation is an "art," less precise, to be learned slowly.

Information Technology (IT) is a key component of many risk-monitoring systems, especially as you approach the realm of dashboard metrics, but Gazzaway cautions that we must not be seduced by the medium at the risk of forgetting the message. There is sometimes a temptation to do something simply because it can be done. So, too, with IT. It is a marvel that can produce wonderful things, but we must always be mindful that it is a medium, and not the message.

Finally, Gazzaway summarizes his observations on the problems he has seen in a career devoted to understanding and mitigation risk. They are two:

1. **Risk changes, and controls do not.** Simply put, we may have controls, carefully developed and finely tuned, to monitor "X," but now have to contend with "Y." The message is that risk mitigation is an adaptive process. We do not do it once, put it in a binder on the bookshelf, and forget it. Like most important things, it is a process.

2. **Risk can stay the same, but the operation of the controls changes.** Again, Gazzaway is emphasizing "balance." Controls may become obsolete, slow, cumbersome, or ineffective (given areas of

risk can grow, shrink, or evolve over time). The controls that worked well five or ten years ago may not be nearly as effective today. This can be to the result of a multitude of "small" factors: responsibility for the controls may have moved from one department to another; a computer platform or a manager may have changed; the regulatory environment may be different; the company may be in a growth or contraction mode it was not in before; there may have been a strategic shift in the focus of the organization; or people may simply have changed or stopped doing what they were doing. In every case, effective monitoring of internal control can identify the change and verify that it is handled properly.

We can learn much from the Trent Gazzaways of the world, who have studied these issues closely. As advisers, they have had the opportunity to see many organizations in many fields over a long period of time and to observe them both in times of prosperity and in times of stress. They have seen what seems to work and also what does not. They have no magic answers. Indeed, simple solutions are often worse than no solution, since they tend to solve the wrong problem or provide a false sense of security, often based on nothing more than the amount of time and energy invested or the amount of money spent. Insight, or, as Gazzaway puts it, "balance," is the key.

SKIP LANGE

E. L. "Skip" Lange has run his own consulting practice, The Touchstone Partnership, for more than fifteen years. Prior to that, he spent five years as a principal and regional practice leader with the professional services firm Laventhol & Horwath. In his current practice, his firm concentrates on strategic management, business process excellence, succession planning, and human resources management and development.

Along the way, he has worked in a number of industries and seen just about everything there is with regard to risk. When asked to recount the primary issues he has encountered related to risk mismanagement, he can respond quickly with a fairly long list of thoughts:

➢ **"Risk is seen as something to be handled by other people."** Note the previous comment by Trent Gazzaway that risk is everyone's job. It is dangerous to think that that if risk is someone else's job, then others in the company need not worry about it.

➢ **"Negative news filters out on its way up. No one wants to be the one to bring shock and disappointment to the boss, and the bigger the boss, the less inclination there is to do it."** This is one of the great benefits of outside consultants. They see a lot of risk and can identify it quickly, but they are not hesitant to tell those in power what they have found. They have an inherent advantage—they don't live there. When their work is done, they can go away. Every now and then a consultant may be inclined to temper her findings in the hope of maintaining a happy atmosphere and possibly getting more work in the future. That is the time to get a new consultant, for you are not getting value for your money.

➢ Consider **"management by walking away."** This is a great line Skip came out with, nicely capturing one of the most powerful sets of human emotions—the tendency to avoid problems and ugliness. We all want to be liked. We don't want to question or offend those we work with, even our subordinates. We don't like dealing with "icky" stuff. We don't want to get people into trouble. We are afraid we might be wrong in our assessment and will look like a fool for even raising the issue. We assume that things will "work out." We allow that things have been like this for a long time, so we just have to live with it. We allow that, while something might not be perfect, so far there haven't been any disasters, so we can go on our way and get back to business. We see the issue, but it's in someone else's department, so we assume they will "handle" it.

Years ago I had a boss, a fairly high-ranking executive, who had a unique theory of management. It went as follows: "If you see ten problems coming down the road, do nothing. Nine of them will run off the road before they hit you." He survived and, indeed, prospered using this unusual management style, but his injunction has some merit, though not perhaps in the manner he meant it. We cannot go to "General Quarters" over every potential issue we find. We will quickly wear the organization out and burn up valuable resources. At the same time, a little problem can grow into a big one fairly quickly. What to do? Analysis, assessment, judgment, and proportional responses seem to work but are frequently not undertaken.

➤ **"Hire good messengers."** Here, Skip is advising that companies hire people who, although on the payroll, can function like outside consultants. They can spot problems and analyze and assess them, and they are not afraid to deliver their findings to those in power. Skip counsels: "Give them the authority to not only spot problems but hold them accountable for bringing them to the appropriate people in management. Most important of all, implement, measure, monitor, and manage risk, holding the people who own the risk accountable."

➤ **"Information Technology (IT) never throws anything away; they might need it someday."** I have seen this problem often in corporations. As I noted in the Introduction, people like me are called in once a problem has been discovered. Often we used the computer forensics people assigned to our fraud and forensic investigations practice. While I am hardly a "computer guy," I am a big fan of computer forensics, which can help you get to the root of a problem fairly quickly. Even those somewhat familiar with the term, however, often misunderstand it. They think it is what they see in the movies or on television—recovering deleted files to find the "smoking e-mail" and doing key-word searches of large databases. That is part of it, but more often it pertains to data mining. When I was with two of the "Big Four" professional services firms, we learned over time to budget about one-third of the total engagement budget for computer forensics. Unfortunately, much of that money was spent cleaning up client electronic data before we could even begin our analysis. I learned to refer to all this electronic junk that is in too many corporate data systems as "background noise." It can be deadly for a couple of reasons: it makes the corporation itself less able to perform meaningful analysis of its own data, and it provides a handy smokescreen for the unscrupulous employee or executive who is trying to play games.

A few examples may be instructive. Several years ago, I had a client that was a major U.S. producer of consumer products. It operated a huge sales center in Europe and had reason to believe there were problems there. The center itself was massive and staffed with hundreds of young people who sat at terminals, wearing headsets and taking orders online or over the phone. The immediate issue quickly became apparent. Because of the way the system was set up, the salesperson could change the unit price of the item at the time he took the order. Thus, an item that was supposed to sell for thirty euros could be sold for two. Pretty quickly, a fair number of the salespeople succumbed to temptation. They could sell things to themselves, their friends, or their family at very deep discounts.

Having worked for two major professional services and accounting firms, I came to learn a bit about accounting. In accounting, there is something called a "low margin report." It is actually pretty simple. You build a product and then price it to produce a certain level of profit. By running low-margin reports, you can quickly determine how you are doing on a given product. Is it producing the expected level of profit?

When we recommended this to the company managers, they shook their heads. Their system would not permit such an analysis. We quickly ascertained the reason. Many multinational corporations are really conglomerates. We think of them as one big company, but actually they are semi-independent companies operating under the same corporate banner throughout the world. If you judged from their buildings and letterheads, you would think these were simply divisions of the parent company, but they are actually quasi-independent contractors.

Because of this structure, and because this sales center took orders from all over Europe, various companies in various countries had various sales incentive programs—"Buy one, get one free!," "20% off for the next ten days!" You get the idea. This company had so much complex and indeed conflicting information in its systems that it had no firm idea of what its margins should be. Thus, any analysis was doomed from the start.

I later saw the same issue with a major multinational pharmaceutical company we were working with on issues of product counterfeiting and gray market sales. It had the same type of multinational umbrella structure. Once, when I was in a meeting with top executives, one ruefully observed the following: "If you asked me today what we sell product X for in country Y, I could tell you. In about ninety days." Left unattended, this kind of situation can result in some bad things.

To go back to Skip and his observations on IT's propensity to hoard data, he counsels having a good data retention policy. Many organizations either do not have one or have one that is seriously out of date. I once found two pallets of important financial records in an off-site storage facility that a bank had simply forgotten it had. There are a number of reasons to have a policy on data retention and for it to be an active, evolving thing: to meet regulatory and legal requirements; to support business operations; to enable the company to defend itself in the event of litigation; to have timely and organized business information; and to promote effective house-keeping.

➤ **"Avoid too much of a clubby atmosphere."** Often those in the "C suite" and on the board of directors become friends. They interact often, are among the top-paid personnel of the corporation, often have similar interests, and may socialize together. All of this is fine, but it may limit their ability to practice truly effective corporate governance and to ask the sometimes hard questions necessary to do so.

➤ **"Avoid senior managers with limited experience, especially in the art of managing."** Many people achieve fairly senior positions largely on their technical expertise. Often they have not gained the necessary range of experience to address more broadly based management responsibilities. Their unintentional "blindness" may lead to problems down the line. This may be a function of mobility. Job-hopping is the norm today, as opposed to the "thirty-five years and a gold watch" that was common half a century ago. Accordingly, a senior manager not only may have limited experience outside her immediate field but may even not know the corporation she works for very well.

➤ **"Who gets stuck with risk? What do you do with risk? It's hard to consider risk an investment."** Therefore, Skip says, risk is often an orphan, shunted to whomever happens to get stuck with it. There are a couple of reasons for this. First of all, it is unclear who owns it in the first place. Second, very few corporate performance plans reward people for avoiding or dealing with risk. We do not think of risk mitigation as an investment the same way we think of mainstream corporate activities.

➢ **"Failure to establish key indicators."** Skip terms these "alert metrics." Most effective companies, he believes, do not need a huge number of key performance and risk indicators, if they have the right ones. Perhaps as few as a half dozen indicators, properly constructed and utilized, will reduce risk exposure significantly.

➢ **"Faulty analysis of information."** We may be looking at data and think we know what we are seeing, but our analysis may be wrong. (Indeed, I have had more than one client make the same complaint: "We are awash in data, but don't have information.") There are two issues here. The first is that we tend to make assumptions about what we are analyzing. If our assumptions are wrong, our analysis is wrong. Second, we may be relying on corrupted data. I once had a client that was a major property casualty insurance company. It had an adjuster go bad. Had she not so obviously displayed signs of wealth in her lifestyle that no one could understand, she might still be running her scheme, which was pretty simple. She was writing checks to herself or her confederates on closed claims. In the insurance business, even an active claim gets relatively little supervisory oversight. A closed claim gets almost none. Thus, a major loophole exists for those inclined to exploit it.

The process, however, is more complex. There is a mantra in the insurance business called "severity." At base, it is pretty simple. Through long years of experience, insurance companies have come to realize that the longer a claim is open, the more it will wind up paying out. Thus, adjusters have a performance metric that requires that they close a certain percentage of their claims each month. This number is watched closely by the top brass and tracked out to the third decimal place. Good numbers mean good business, or so they think. Getting these claims closed in time to hit the metric is not always easy to do, but since the adjusters want to keep their boss off their back, they close claims prematurely. There is no fraud involved; they are simply "playing the game." Thus, they often write legitimate checks on legitimate claims after the date the claim was supposedly closed.

When we discovered this adjuster's scheme we went to the company's director of security, who was a former police detective commander and a long-time veteran of the insurance business. We asked a fairly simple question: did the company ever run exception reports? An exception report in this instance would be "date of check after date claim closed." Pretty simple stuff. He smiled, perhaps suspecting where we were going, and replied that he did and that he had run one last month. We asked what the results were, and he replied, "Thirty-seven thousand." We assumed that meant dollars and asked him about it. He again replied simply, "No. Checks."

Thirty-seven thousand checks had been paid on closed claims in a single month. These employees were not stealing; they were "playing the game" to keep their bosses happy but, in so doing, created so much background noise that it made it easier for someone inclined to steal to do so. It also made it more difficult to pick up their activities, since so many misleading data were being generated. This demonstrates the danger of bad data management practices, but it also highlights an area little utilized by most corporations. I suggest to internal and external auditors that they start their audits in human resources. Pull the performance plans and take note of the performance metrics of various employees. People will try to hit those metrics to keep their bosses happy, but, in so doing, they may create an environment ripe for problems. Why? Anyone who has a perform-ance plan—so many goods sold, so many items produced—has both financial and psychological incentives to achieve those numbers. Do people sometimes "fudge" to get there? Yes, and doing so can cause unintended problems.

"Nobody questions good news." This is a problem I have seen over and over, and it can be deadly. At the end of this chapter, I recount some startling examples of this. They may seem unbelievable, but I assure you they are true.

DAVE VANNORT

CPA Dave Vannort was a "career" guy with the multinational, multi-billion-dollar professional services and accounting firm Deloitte & Touche LLP (D&T). Dave spent thirty-three years there, the last twenty-two as a partner in charge of D&T's offices in Greenville and Columbia, South Carolina. Throughout his career, he pretty much saw it all and conducted or managed thousands of audits and other professional service engagements.

Just when he thought he was ready for retirement, a new chal-lenge and opportunity called, from an old friend and old client—SCANA. The name does not really stand for anything; rather, it is the name of the holding company for South Carolina Electric & Gas, a huge energy and power company that, at the present time, has grown beyond South Carolina in the energy and power sector.

As Dave tells the story, one day the general counsel of SCANA gave the chief executive officer (CEO) a briefing on the provisions of the federal sentencing guidelines (FSG) for organizations. FSG, which were fairly new at the time, reflected the federal government's firm intent to deal harshly with corporations and their executives when they ran afoul of the law. The CEO listened intently and decided on the spot that he, SCANA, and his successor (he was getting close to retirement) would not be subject to these penalties if they could help it.

Thus it was that Dave was contacted and asked to leave his brief "retirement" to come to SCANA and head up its compliance office. SCANA already had compliance programs in place; indeed, D&T had played a role in updating and coordinating these. Dave's job was to pull it all together and make sure all the potential issues were covered. Dave accepted the offer, with one condition—he wanted to work only an additional two years. SCANA agreed, as both it and Dave thought an updated and comprehensive program could be created in that time.

Dave completed his task on time. He owed his success to a number of factors:

➤ **Solid Top-Side Support.** When Dave took the job, he became vice president for corporate compliance, but his was not the typical vice president's position. He reported to only two people, and it would be difficult to find two persons more powerful in any organization—the CEO and the chairman of the audit committee of the board of directors. Dave and these two executives set the groundwork for success—support from the very top.

➤ **A Clear Plan Aimed at Completion of the Project.** Dave did not have a huge infrastructure—his budget was $1 million per year, and he had but one person on his staff, but he had a plan rarely seen in corporations. First, because of their valuable work to date, he retained and expanded the D&T team and tasked it with a fifteen-month project to complete and refine the compliance work it had already done. He mandated a turn-key job—that is, when the team was finished, the program would be fully documented, articulated, and operational.

Dave also established a hotline for employees, the SCANA Compliance Helpline, which was staffed by a professional outside provider. Dave went two steps further than many corporations: (1) he expanded the hotline to make it available to customers and vendors; and (2) he and his staff actively tested the hotline on a periodic basis, making anonymous calls to report contrived events to see how quickly and accurately they were reported. Few corporations do this, but it is an excellent idea. The existence and availability of the hotline were advertised daily to employees through monthly posters, the weekly newsletter, a hotline calendar, and any other media the corporate communications department could think of to keep the hotline visible to anyone in the company.

➢ **An Updated Code of Conduct.** At the time, SCANA had 4,000 employees and twenty senior executives. As a corporation, it had had a few run-ins with federal regulators—nothing huge, but troublesome nonetheless. As the program began to roll out, the long-standing corporate Code of Conduct was updated to reflect the nature of SCANA's current operations and also to advise of new risks arising in the company's operating environment. The updated code was written in a user-friendly format with the underlying message "Always Do The Right Thing" emphasized throughout. Dave announced that all 4,000 employees would be trained on the requirements and responsibilities of the new compliance program and the new Code of Conduct. That was not too controversial; everyone expected it at some point or another. What SCANA did next, with the full support of the CEO and chairman of the audit committee, did cause heads to turn.

➤ **Use of Senior Executives as Trainers.** SCANA's chief operating officer (COO) advised the twenty senior executives that they were personally responsible for training their employees. All of them. There was to be no delegation; the senior executives had to do the training in person, for hours at a time, until everyone had successfully completed the program.

As one might imagine, at first there was some resistance and push-back, followed by pleas referring to schedules already full, but the prior support of the CEO and the audit committee chairman and now the CEO in Training made it obvious that there would be no excuses. As things turned out, these executives morphed into superb trainers, and what better message to send the rank and file that the boss was 100 percent on board and fully conversant with the compliance program? To make sure, Dave drove all over the state of South Carolina (SCANA has operations in numerous locations) to sit in on these training sessions and monitor how they were going. He spent a lot of time on the road, but the idea that the eyes of the big guys were on those senior executives as they conducted the training programs infused them with a sense of energy and urgency.

Dave completed his task in the time agreed to, and SCANA had a modern, comprehensive compliance program. But implementing a world-class program is neither easy nor automatic. Even with the benefit of solid support from top management, Dave still had a lot of work to do. However, without such support, his task would have been well-nigh impossible.

The lesson to be learned is that each corporation is unique in its own way, and there is no easy answer to effective implementation. Judgment and experience are key elements in achieving success.

Even after guiding a large, complex organization to a position of compliance strength, an old pro like Dave still grapples with the key question: *who owns risk?* Dave admits that there is no easy answer. Depending on the corporation, it could be a "C suite" executive, the board of directors, the audit committee, a risk committee, or some other person or entity. He also notes that few corporations have a chief risk officer, and, even among those that do, a standard definition of the scope of their responsibilities is lacking.

Perhaps, at some point in the future, the responsibility for managing risk within a corporation will be more firmly defined, but, for the time being, the old pros like Dave, working with solid topside support, seem to be the best answer.

KEN FRIEDMAN

For a man only in his forties, Ken Friedman has seen a lot of corporate woe in his career as an attorney. Following many years at the firm of Dewey Ballantine LLP, he moved to Manatt, Phelps & Phillips LLP, in Manhattan. When asked about his experience in dealing with corporate legal issues, he had a number of observations.

➢   **Look more closely at the shop-floor level.** The general counsel (GC) normally sees the corporation from the level of the "C suite," much like the CEO. That, in Friedman's term, is the "35,000-foot view." Friedman counsels that someone also needs to be looking at the 5,000-foot level, where problems can be detected early and dealt with while they still are of manageable size. By the time these issues can be seen from 35,000 feet, they are, by definition, big issues. Often, Friedman advises, the GC usually lives in a world of "Whose hair is burning?" That is, they frequently tend to act as a manager of problems, rather than a manager of risk. Again, this results in part from the self-perception of the position and in part from the fact that no one seems to be looking at what is going on from 5,000 feet. Or, as Friedman puts it, "No one is seeing what is happening at the shop-floor level."

➤ **Monitor industry developments.** Friedman also notes that many GCs tend not to look sideways. It is the old "ABC" model—do we have a bad apple, a bad bushel, or a bad crop? The tendency is to deal with the bad apple and, since there are no other known instances we can see from 35,000 feet, to assume that the rest of the bushel and the crop are fine. Friedman recommends horizontal scanning. Problems tend to run in industries; each industry has its own particular variety. The wise GC, he believes, will closely monitor industry developments and issues and determine if issues that occur at similar organizations might also be affecting her corporation.

➤ **Practice preemptive risk management where possible.** GCs are often on the hot seat, since people tend to dump problems on their desks. Generally, they do not see themselves, nor does the corporation see them, as the chief risk officer. Indeed, everyone in the "C suite" sort of assumes that someone else is performing that role or that each executive has a share of risk responsibility and that, if the company is lucky, they will overlap enough so that nothing important slips through the cracks. Compounding this problem is the age-old tendency not to deliver bad news; as Friedman puts it, "Contrary views are not welcome."

This is an interesting proposition. While, in most corporate structures, no one person clearly owns risk, once the litigation starts to fly everyone owns risk. Lawsuits are notorious for naming multiple officials and officers of the corporation, with the result that those who believed risk was not their job or at least not a very big part of it must face the task of defending themselves on the basis of that very assumption.

The most common form of preemptive risk management practiced by many corporations, Friedman believes, is having contracts reviewed in advance by attorneys knowledgeable in the field in question. Friedman, for example, has wide experience in the transportation and construction industries (which are notorious for the litigation they spawn), and he can often advise clients on ways to insert more careful or precise wording, thus reducing their risk. This, however, seems to him to be the exception to an otherwise resigned risk management position of "let's deal with it when it happens."

This, indeed, is a major challenge for a GC function already swamped with work and striving endlessly to hold down outside legal costs. To take on the responsibility of being the chief risk officer is probably too daunting. So the parade marches on, with various departments and corporate functions assuming that someone else will handle risk, that everyone is handling his share, and that the parts will come together to equal the whole or, perhaps more common, that, since nothing has happened that management is aware of, there isn't any significant level of risk.

Attorneys like Friedman can only counsel that that can be a very risky assumption.

FRED VERINDER

Fred Verinder earned his nickname of "Freddy the Fabulous Federal Ferret" early on in his FBI career for his aggressive, never-give-up style and for his prodigious work ethic. As a CPA, he naturally spent a fair amount of his time working white-collar crime cases.

As time went on and he moved up the ranks, he commanded an FBI field office before returning to FBI Headquarters as a deputy assistant director in the Criminal Investigative Division. Again, he was in charge of white-collar crime, this time for the entire FBI. During this period, the savings and loan crisis was raging and the health care industry was coming under serious investigation. When time came for his retirement, he naturally gravitated to what he knew, accepting a position with a health care company as director of compliance, then later moving to the Council of Ethical Organizations, a not-for-profit.

His last job came unexpectedly. He thought he was in a state of semiretirement after leaving his previous job when he got a call from Blue Cross/Blue Shield of Illinois. The name is a little misleading, as that corporate entity (it went through several name changes) also managed health care programs in several other states. The company had been the subject of a federal investigation and had negotiated a plea agreement and paid a substantial fine, but it was barred from participating in some federal programs—not good news, considering the amount of funding the federal government pours into the health care system.

The company had learned of Fred and his reputation and wanted him to come in and get the operation into compliance. Fred, taken by the challenge and the substantial salary being offered, reconsidered retirement and went back to work. On the basis of his prior experience and of what he learned in this position (he got the company back to gold-standard levels), he offers the following observations and recommendations to any company concerned about its risk compliance programs meant to mitigate risk.

> **Get the buy-in of the board.** In the BC/BS case, this was not too hard, considering the rocky time the company had recently gone

through, but Verinder counsels that it is a critical first step. With the board's support, he had an absolute mandate to address anything he saw that was out of kilter. Without such firm support, many compliance directors live in a continual state of frustration. That this is so makes sense. Compliance programs cost money and tie up employees' time. They may be seen as slowing down or interfering with operations in a highly competitive marketplace.

➤ **Employees must be trained, empowered, and protected.** The training is necessary to ensure that they fully understand the consequences of acts they or others commit. The potential issues and likely consequences of such acts must be made clear to them. They must be encouraged to "do the right thing" and to report any suspected violations, using an anonymous hotline, if they wish. Then they must be assured that no retaliation of any kind will befall them for bringing a concern to the attention of management. Only with these three elements in place can employees act as the eyes and ears of the compliance program. Failure to have such mechanisms in place can quickly doom any compliance program, no matter how well crafted.

At first, Verinder outsourced the training function, but, as his staff gained experience, he gradually developed a cadre of in-house trainers. In-house personnel have several advantages: they are cheaper; they know the company and its operations better; and they are more readily accepted as "one of us."

One function he did continue to outsource was investigations. Each time an allegation was received, it was investigated. If remedial action was needed, it was taken. If rules and procedures needed to be changed, they were changed. There are a number of advantages to using outside resources, usually former federal agents. First, they are available only when needed. Second, they have vast experience in the proper conduct and documentation of an investigation. Third, they have seen pretty much everything in their careers and often spot a problem quickly. Last, being outsiders they have the inherent advantage of being able to ask the sometimes tough questions, even of the powerful, that an in-house employee might find awkward.

➤ **You must analyze risk.** What has happened in the past? What is happening in the industry? What do professionals in other companies see? What standards are recommended by professional associations? (Among other groups, Verinder was a member of the Ethics Officers Association.) What is being written about? What are government hearings and studies disclosing? Compliance is a dynamic process, and it can grow stale and ineffective if not updated and monitored.

➤ **The Compliance Committee must have the proper mix of people.** Certainly, the CEO, CFO, and general counsel are obvious members, but Fred counsels that it is wise to also have managers from the various operating departments and divisions, lest they begin to believe that compliance is someone else's job.

➤ **Identify the primary and most important risks.** Verinder advises that some companies may have a hundred areas of risk. While all need to be tended to, he counsels that it is wise to pay particular attention to the top twenty. If everything is a number one priority, nothing really is, and the compliance program can suffer.

➤ **Involve the internal audit staff and make them aware of issues to look for in the conduct of their work.** Verinder advised that, in addition to an internal audit team, he developed small teams of five or six people in divisions with the greatest risk potential. After receiving special training, these teams were tasked with conducting quarterly audits of their divisions.

➤ **Publicize the program, and make it available both online and in written materials.** Provide it to both vendors and customers, with clear examples of the program's objectives and telephone numbers to call to report any concerns.

The biggest risk of all, Verinder believes, is to have a compliance program and then "put it on the shelf." He believes that if it is going to be effective, it has to be a living, dynamic process that adapts to changes both in the environment and within the company.

"FAST EDDIE"

When one enters the small, but bustling, coastal town of Shalotte, in southeastern North Carolina, it takes but a short turn off the main road to see a tall sign, emblazoned with the famed star-shaped Texaco logo that says "Express Lube." A smaller sign to the left of the door of the neat, tidy building is more descriptive. It says "Fast Eddie's, Express Lube, Plus."

As you approach, you do not find what you might expect from a normal "car" place. On the left side of the building there is a spacious outside seating area for customers, furnished with plastic and wicker tables and chairs. Inside there is a customer waiting area with a coffee table, comfortable chairs, magazines, newspapers, and a television set. Restrooms and complimentary coffee are nearby.

Edward "Fast Eddie" Gartner is a man who has earned his nickname. In simple terms, Fast Eddie is a "car guy." Always has been, always will be. As a kid, he tinkered with cars, tuned them, rebuilt them, bought and sold them, and raced them. It was logical that, as an adult, he would go into the car business, eventually rising to being the parts and service manager of several major car dealerships in New Jersey.

As the years passed, Fast Eddie learned and excelled at his trade. But, eventually, the lure of warmer weather, fishing, and being in NASCAR country proved to be too much. He moved to Shalotte, in the Cape Fear region.

At work, he is, as his nickname implies, a blur of motion. He is a sturdy man, with a shaved head and reading glasses perched on the tip of his nose or the top of his forehead. He is always moving, answering the phone, greeting customers, ordering parts, and, most important, checking the four service bays to see how his service technicians are doing. On these forays, he is constantly monitoring the progress of work and asking questions about his workers' diagnoses of the customers' car problems. Drawing on his knowledge, developed through many years in the field, he often suggests short cuts to solving a customer problem or recommends a more detailed diagnostic test that should be done to get at the heart of the issue.

Like any businessman, Fast Eddie has to pay his bills and make a profit, but he is not out to maximize his income. His first priority is to serve his customers. If he does that, the profits will follow. I am a classic case in point. I drive an eight-year-old Cadillac DeVille, which I bought used coming off a two-year lease. The car had been well maintained, had reasonable mileage, and still had many years and miles left on the factory warranty. I'm fairly tall and a pack rat, so I always like big, comfortable cars with lots of trunk space.

When I first came to Fast Eddie for a simple oil change, he took the time to get to know a little about me, the DeVille, my use of it, and my expectations for it. Over the years, this has paid off in real dollars, since from time to time Eddie will discover a problem with the vehicle. His advice is always sound, for the problem may be serious ("Joe, this is going to be a problem in a couple of thousand miles, and you probably ought to get it taken care of before you break down on the road") or not-so-serious ("Joe, this is starting to go, but it isn't a safety issue and, considering the age of the car, if you can live with it. I wouldn't bother messing with it.").

As I began this book, I resolved to interview Fast Eddie. I had seen his management style in Shalotte, but I wondered about his experience as the parts and service manager at those New Jersey dealerships. Surely, he had trained scores, if not hundreds, of young service technicians. How did he do it? When I asked the question, Eddie responded instantly with only three words: "Clear your mind."

Readers may find it strange that I include Fast Eddie in a "management" book about risk mitigation. (For what it is worth, Fast Eddie did, also.) However, I think we have valuable lessons to learn from the "Fast Eddies" of the world when we are thinking about risk. Here are the three most important points:

1. **Get out and look around.** I mentioned that Fast Eddie is a blur of motion. In management terms, we dress that up and call it MBWA (Management by Walking Around). Many fabled corporate executives have been written up and complimented for employing this management style. Not relying totally on computer-generated reports and "executive summaries" that may leave out important details, they frequently wander the shop floor, the loading dock, and the office cubicles to see what is going on, to see it, taste it, and smell it. Often they can glean valuable information from a casual comment, a blank stare (someone isn't aware of an important new policy that had gone out as top priority to all employees), or a caustic remark. All of these are valuable sources of information, for they indicate how things are, as opposed to how you think they are or how they "should" be.

2. **Determine what is critical and what is not.** Fast Eddie took the time to meet me and to understand my tolerance for risk as the driver of an older vehicle. He felt an obligation to recommend important, safety-related repairs but also advised me that more minor cosmetic repairs on a vehicle that age probably were not worth the money. This is an important lesson for executives facing risk. All-encompassing programs to deal with every risk the corporation may face are fine, but they take a lot of time and cost a lot of money. It is important to know what you really need to do and equally important to understand areas of risk that you can safely ignore or that at worst may cause but a minor problem if and when they go bad. Thank you, Fast Eddie.

3. **Clear your mind.** The third element, the three words, was probably Fast Eddie's most valuable contribution. "Clear you mind" should be the approach any executive, regardless of organizational rank, takes to the news of any problem. What Fast Eddie was trying to teach his young service technicians was to listen and understand, and not jump to conclusions. In the car service business, as in the corporate world, this is always a temptation. We are pressed for time, and are rightfully proud of our long and hard-earned experience, but if we jump too soon we may land on the wrong conclusion and waste valuable time and money chasing the wrong problem.

THE DANGERS OF NOT QUESTIONING GOOD NEWS

As promised earlier in this chapter, here are some examples I have run across in my work in risk management of companies that put too much faith in good news and paid for it later.

The Credit Card Company

I once did work for a credit card company that had experienced problems with a senior financial executive. In the course of our work, we had occasion to interview the president of a captive bank the credit card outfit had purchased to receive and process its credit card payments. The president of the bank was a person in his early forties, with no college degree and no financial background (I know, because I always check the personnel file before I conduct an interview). You could not see the walls of his rather spacious office. They were covered with awards and plaques, photographs of him with the bank chairman at annual awards banquets, and glowing letters attesting to his good and faithful service and his remarkable achievements.

The interview went fine, but I was curious about all the awards. This person seemed cordial, but I did not have the sense that he was a financial whiz of any sort. Back I went to human resources, where I asked if the awards had been accompanied by memoranda justifying them. Sure enough, a file was produced. I glanced through it and made some notes, but I could not believe what I was seeing. For example, the bank had about ninety-some accounts holding almost $900 million in credit card debt. This person's performance metric for two years prior for bad debt write-offs was to hold write-offs to $750,000, a pretty low number for that much credit card debt. He held it to $5,000. The next year, his write-off target was $500,000, again a very low number. He brought it in at year end at $250. Those numbers are right; I did not drop any zeros at the end of that number.

This struck me as beyond comprehension. The attorney I was working with and I later interviewed this person and, per my interview notes, asked him the same question for eight minutes. The question was simple: how were you able to achieve such incredibly low write-off rates on so much debt? Finally, he allowed that maybe, possibly, perhaps you could do it by moving bad debt between accounts, thereby giving it a fresh ninety-day life until it became due again and had to be moved again. He had been doing this for years, nobody had paid any attention, and the plaques and awards kept piling up. Our client started off with a potential problem employee and wound up coming to realize that it was sitting on a tidal wave of bad debt. Impossible, you say? What about senior management, the internal and external auditors, the audit committee, and the board of directors? I don't know how all those safeguards seemed not to work. All I know is what I saw. Lest you think this was a one-in-a-million case, let me provide a couple more examples.

The Manufacturer

Our client was the audit committee of a large, publicly traded company. It had foreign ownership, U.S. corporate headquarters, and nine operating facilities around the country. The CEO decided he was going to be a star, so he took the budgets and profit plans created in the normal course of business and "stretched" them. The new goals were not only ambitious; they were highly unlikely to be met. He solved that problem by instructing his CFO to "hit the numbers." The CFO also realized there was no reasonable way this was going to happen, so, under pressure, he began getting inventive with his accounting, but this required the assistance of the corporate comptroller. This man, also a financial professional, realized that the numbers were unachievable, but he also felt the pressure that was trickling down. He, in turn, had to instruct the nine plant comptrollers as to how they would record revenue and expenses.

These folks recognized what was going on. Nothing had ever been put in writing or written in an e-mail, but phone calls and site visits from corporate officials got the message across loud and clear. The plant controllers, too, had jobs they were trying to hold onto, but they felt offended by the nature and intent of what they were being forced to participate in, so they decided to rebel in a quiet manner. Each quarter for almost four years, each of the nine plants came in within $100 of budget. The fact that this was well-nigh impossible never seemed to catch the attention of any of the watchdogs, until one day it all blew up.

I could go on all day, but I will stop after one more.

The Wholesaler

Once again, working with outside counsel, I was involved in an internal investigation. The company was foreign-owned, with U.S. corporate headquarters. It had eleven locations around the country in major cities and was a wholesaler of office products. Business seemed to be good, but the CEO in one particular city was consistently able to achieve profit margins 15 percent higher than those achieved in any of the other locations, although the regions were identical in almost every way. One would think that the normal corporate reaction would be to study this success carefully and try to replicate it in the other ten cities, but this did not happen. Then, one day someone cried "foul!"

Our investigation confirmed the same old story—an overaggressive CEO had forced his CFO and financial reporting folks to cook the books to make him a superstar. Indeed, he was a superstar. He lived in a mansion, drove an expensive car, and belonged to a very high-end country club. When the folks from corporate came to visit his city, they were met at the airport by Mercedes limousines, whisked to lavish suites at the best hotels, and wined and dined at the finest restaurants. Money was no object.

When we met with the audit committee to report our preliminary findings, a number of corporate executives were also present, including the CFO. After we had established from our analysis of the books and records how this amazing financial performance had been achieved, someone posed a question to the corporate CFO: didn't he think this track record of financial success was a bit out of the ordinary? This gentleman sighed and said, "Yeah, but we just loved seeing the numbers."

Believe me, there are more examples, but the message I am trying to get across is simple: good news can kill you.

processes in place. These may vary, depending upon the corporate and financial structure of the organization, the industry in which it operates, and the disposition of its board of directors and executive officers. It may be instructive to look at how a few corporations deal with these issues. Let's start with some of the ideas unearthed by Bill Parrett in his excellent book on corporate governance and risk.

EXECUTIVE PERSPECTIVES ON RISK

Bill Parrett went about as high as you can go in the global "Big Four" professional services firm of Deloitte & Touche LLP (D&T). He held just about every job, managed thousands of professional employees, dealt with hundreds of corporate CEOs, boards of directors, and audit committees, and saw just about every industry and service organization there is. In his 2007 book, *The Sentinel CEO: Perspectives on Security, Risk, and Leadership in a Post-9/11 World*, he makes a number of personal observations and also portrays the reflections of the many CEOs he dealt with over the years. First, however, he makes a telling point, mentioned earlier in this book, about the incredibly broad scope of the term "risk." It is quite simple. Despite the many tools available and the many bright consultants eager to explain, install, and implement them—Enterprise Risk Management (ERM) is one of the older and more popular—there is no standard definition of "risk." Each corporation and each executive must figure this out for himself.[1] (Recall the comments of Trent Gazzaway in Chapter 3 to the effect that "one size does not fit all.")

In addition to his own observations, Parrett also provides some examples of how the many CEOs he has dealt with have approached the issue of risk in the manner seemingly best suited to their corporations and circumstances. Here are two of his key findings:

1. Redundancy in oversight costs more, but, depending upon the nature of the risk and regulatory environment, it is worth the investment.[2]
2. Recovery plans must be based on operational, and not theoretical, assumptions.[3]

Parrett's firm, D&T, sponsored many surveys around the world each year and shared the results with clients and potential clients. One survey of the 100 companies that had suffered the greatest declines in share price during the period 1996–2003 attempted to determine the cause for the lost value. Using the Committee of Sponsoring Organizations (COSO) framework as a guide, D&T grouped its findings into four broad categories:

1. Strategic risks (e.g., demand shortfalls, execution, impact of competition)
2. Operational risks (e.g., cost controls, supply chain issues)
3. Financial risk (e.g., debt trading losses)
4. External risks (e.g., political, economic, industry issues)[4]

In ruminating about these findings, Parrett makes a telling observation: many of these companies were impacted when two or more risk factors hit them at the same time. [5] (While we tend to focus on one specific risk, then another, we rarely plan or allow for the impact of two or more risks occurring simultaneously, thereby creating a multiplier effect. During my final years in the FBI, one of things I was responsible for was a large fleet of aircraft used to support various FBI operations. Although I was not a pilot, I had many skilled pilots working for me, and, because of my position, I would chair the Accident Review Board, which convened whenever we had an aircraft accident. One of the things that struck me about those meetings was that most accidents were not caused by one big thing that went wrong. They were caused by two or three smaller things that went wrong at the same time.)

Parrett goes on to provide other real-life examples of risk that was not properly anticipated or managed and suggests prudent steps that can be taken to better manage it:

> ➤ Careful merging of support or back-office operations; too-rapid consolidation has a negative impact upon production and customer-relations operations.
> ➤ The creation of chief security officer (CSO) positions, which brings various corporate security issues under the purview of one executive.
> ➤ Cultivation of a more holistic approach to the issue of risk management, including the development of more effective information management systems.
> ➤ Testing of risk models by subjecting them to hypothetical rare events.
> ➤ Establishment of a continuing debate and dialog about the most useful and accurate definition of the popular terms "enterprise risk management" (ERM) and "business continuity planning" (BCP).
> ➤ Appreciation and further refinement of the distinction between providing abundant data and presenting only critical information needed by top decision makers. (Note the comments elsewhere in this book made to me over the years by a number of clients to the effect of "We are data rich, and information poor").
> ➤ Efforts to gain a better appreciation of and ability to utilize risk metrics that are not easily quantified.
> ➤ Learning to better appreciate the nonfinancial performance of executives and managers who manage risk.[6]

This summary hardly does justice to the scope of Parrett's thinking and insights, but I hope it provides a glimpse of where some forward-thinking risk executives are going. His entire book is recommended.

ADVANCE UNTIL FIRED UPON—A PHILOSOPHY OF RISK

Risk has many nuances and, as many experts (including Parrett) have noted, means different things to different people in different fields of endeavor. This, in turn, means that rarely do two corporations approach their risk issues in exactly the same manner. All too often they use an approach well described by the consultant, writer, and theorist Karl Albrecht in his book *The Northbound Train*, in which Albrecht discusses corporations and how they scan their environments for both risk and opportunity. He recounts an amusing, but instructive, story about his days in the military. The training group he was in had senior officers (often referred to as "tactical" officers) as instructors/advisors/evaluators. It was fairly common practice to rotate leadership roles among the trainees, often on short notice, to see how they would assess their tactical situation (say, attacking a hill) and react. In one exercise, Albrecht recounts, one of his classmates was designated the new, temporary leader. Somewhat flustered and aware he was under the watchful scrutiny of the tactical officers, the young man thought about his situation for a brief period, then issued his "order" to his "troops." The order was "Advance until fired upon."[7]

Albrecht notes that this is not a very comprehensive plan for dealing with risk, in this case the chance of being shot at by the enemy, but he observes that it is all too often the "strategy" corporations adopt when facing possible risk. In my words, not Albrecht's, it boils down to this: "Let's keep doing what we're doing, and see if anything bad happens. Then we'll deal with it."

RETURN ON INVESTMENT AND RISK COST

Bill Parrett, whose comments I have already set forth, makes a telling suggestion about why even well-run corporations full of bright,
motivated people might avoid dealing with risk: they have a hard
time grappling with the return on investment (ROI) issue. What is
the right amount to spend to avoid risk? What do we get back for
these expenditures? From internal audit to external audit, from corporate security to IT security and crisis management planning, corporations have struggled for many years to establish the "payback"
they get from such activities. This is tougher to measure than things
like sales and production.[8]

There is no easy answer to the question of how much to spend
to manage risk, but in my experience (again, I dealt mainly with
"train wrecks" after things went wrong), most corporations err on
the side of paying too little attention to risk issues. A case in point
is an inquiry I was involved in during my post-FBI career. The company in question was a multibillion-dollar, multinational company
that was under investigation by several authorities for possible violations of the Foreign Corrupt Practices Act (FCPA, the law that
makes it a federal crime to bribe a foreign official for the purpose of
getting business). The audit committee saw a need to act swiftly and
decisively, and the company retained two major law firms. A short
time later, the firm I worked for was retained to assist the attorneys.
My partner and I made numerous trips around the world to review
records and conduct interviews. Each trip, between the fees our firm
charged and the travel cost, was expensive, and we made a lot of
them.

About a year into the inquiry, there was a conference call with
the audit committee to discuss the status of the work to date. My
partner and I called in and were placed on speaker phone. The meet-

ing lasted well over three hours. The committee members were there, senior executives from the firm were there, the two law firms were there, and we were there, albeit by telephone. As these things tend to happen, there were lulls in the discussions, during which the people present tended to talk to one another, unmindful of the fact that the speaker phone was still on. During one of these interludes, one committee member remarked to another, "You know, this thing has already cost us $100 million."

The number is correct—$100 million! Corporations may get anxious about the ROI for resources devoted to risk management since such investment does not seem to contribute to the bottom line, but when something bad hits, the checkbook flies open and the bottom-line impact can be severe. And this was well before the corporation's day of reckoning with the authorities. Still, $100 million can buy a lot of risk management.

I understand the quandary corporate executives face. I have called on them often to discuss preventive risk measures, and my efforts, by and large, have been futile. I, and people like me, tend to get called when the house in on fire. The executives' reaction is not dismissive or illogical; they often say something like "You're the third person in the last two days that wants to sell me something to reduce risk. If I listened to all of you guys, I wouldn't get out of bed in the morning."

This is a fair point. When I referred to a squirrel that spent half its time scanning for risk, I was using a real, but extreme, example, No corporation can afford to spend half its resources scanning or managing risk—it would soon go out of business. But, at least in my experience, too few spend enough on risk-related activities, whatever the percentage may turn out to be.

Even as a "risk professional," I realize that corporations must be prudent with their expenditures, and I can cite an old story in law enforcement to reinforce that fact. The story concerns a fictional chief of police who appeared before the town board with his annual budget request. The old chief had two versions of his presentation. Version one was "Crime is up, so we need more money and more people." The second was "Crime is down and what we're doing is working, so we need more money and more people to keep it from creeping back up." Pick the one you like.

I recently called a former Big Four colleague, still working as a semiretired consultant. I caught him at a bad time; he had a report to get out on a corporate legal matter. Although I had not worked on this issue, I was well aware of it, as he and a number of my other Big Four associates had been working on it for some time. I remarked that, while I understood his time constraints, I was surprised that the matter had not been resolved. His reply was both simple and telling: "Hell, this thing has been going on for six years and four months now."

Risk, misunderstood or misdiagnosed, can be expensive. This case did not involve a "name" matter you might have seen on the Internet or television or read about in *The Wall Street Journal* or the *New York Times*. It might have rated a line or two at some point, but any media coverage of it was mainly local. And it certainly did not reach the $100 million level. It nevertheless represented a significant outlay for a small company that made a poor decision about risk.

GETTING DOWN TO THE BASICS

Many of the leading authorities on risk management speak the same language, although in somewhat different terms. There are prudent steps to take in contemplating and dealing with risk, and they are hardly state secrets. In *Internal Auditing: Assurance and Consulting*

Services, Kurt Reding and colleagues provide some comprehensive checklists of steps to take. A partial list of their recommendations and observations includes:

> ➢ Have the appropriate governance structure in place.
> ➢ Ensure an appropriate level of independence for those in risk assessment positions.
> ➢ Clearly define responsibilities.
> ➢ Provide adequate authority to those responsible for risk management.
> ➢ Design a logical reporting scheme, based on the size and nature of risk.
> ➢ Reevaluate the risk process periodically to make sure it is up to date and meets the expectations of stakeholders and regulators.
> ➢ Ensure that delegated responsibilities are clearly understood.
> ➢ Identify the organizational processes and activities that support the risk management infrastructure.
> ➢ Establish a risk committee.
> ➢ Ensure that all key risks are identified.
> ➢ Ensure the integrity and timeliness of information.[9]

In thinking about the ROI issue and the proper amount of resources to devote to managing a particular risk or set of risks, Reding and his associates recommend a three-phase process:

1. Estimate the potential severity of the risk.
2. Estimate the likelihood, or incidence, of the risk.
3. Consider the best and most effective steps to manage the risk.[10]

Here we get to a simple principle, or, as Trent Gazzaway puts it, "balance." We cannot go full bore at every potential problem we sense. At the same time, if we do not understand our risk environment very well and "advance until fired upon," we run the chance of ignoring considerable risk. The answer lies in information, judgment as to priorities, and effective management strategies. This probably sounds simple and rudimentary, but it is the base line of all risk analysis. The foundation of the base line is information (not data, which can only cloud the horizon). Some may ask, "Fine, but where is the formula? What's the equation we can plug into our computer systems to tell us what is important, how we should rank it, and how we should deal with it?" Many systems and approaches can help with this, but ultimately it comes down to judgment based upon study and experience. Even that may sometimes fail, but, without it, risk looms large.

Having said that, I must add that any number of risk mechanisms are part of the everyday landscape of the typical corporation. A cursory recounting of them will provide some sense of their scope and diversity:

➢ The corporate legal structure is designed to minimize risk. Many corporations are legally based in Delaware, although they may have little or no physical presence there, since the laws of that small state provide a better corporate risk venue than those of other states.

➢ Depending upon the corporate format and industry, various regulatory bodies may watch over the corporation's affairs. Reports must be filed, and procedures must conform to certain sets of requirements.

➢ The board of directors sits atop all this corporate activity; its members are, one hopes, experienced, wise, inquisitive, active, and knowing.

➢ The audit committee of the board (AC) drills deep into management style and practices, accounting issues, and any potentially significant deviation from policy. It also monitors the performance (in most cases) of both the internal and external audit functions.

➤ The chief financial officer (CFO) keeps an eye on the corporate financial operations, ensures that ratios crucial to various loan covenants are maintained, plans fiscal strategy, and deals with cash management and credit risk issues and other financial considerations.

➤ The chief operating officer (COO) keeps the place running, dealing with issues from supply chain management to staffing to production schedules.

➤ The chief information officer (CIO) is usually the executive in charge of the technology/computer infrastructure of the organization.

➤ The chief audit executive (CAE), also sometimes called the director of internal audit, is responsible for the planning and execution of the annual internal audit plan and, usually, the investigation of any discrepancies found.

➤ The chief security officer (CSO) is responsible for many areas, including the safety of the parking lot or garage; perimeter security; visitor and access control; protection of people, property, and inventory; protection of intellectual property; disaster preparedness; and executive protection.

➤ The external auditors must conduct at least an annual audit to be able to opine on the financial and operational health of the corporation.

➤ Depending upon the nature of the corporation's mission, any number of other officials might be engaged, from fire safety to environmental protection to customs and trade experts.

The point is that corporations are not dismissive of risk—they tend to pay a lot of attention to it—but failures still occur with surprising frequency. Why? There are several possible reasons.

LITTLE THINGS MEAN A LOT

The legendary college football coach Joe Paterno, of Penn State, once said the following: "You are never as good as you look when you win, and you are never as bad as you look when you lose."

His message is both profound and simple. The margin between victory and defeat is often quite small. So, too, with risk—the difference between success and failure can often be very small.

Sports talk show host Mike Francesa once made this point in one of his broadcasts while talking about baseball. These are not his exact words, but they capture accurately the flavor of what he meant: "In any given season, the best team in baseball will lose one-third of its games. And in the same season, the worst team in baseball will win one-third of its games. It's the middle third that makes the difference."

This becomes readily apparent if one thinks about competitive sports. Many baseball and hockey games, at whatever level, are won by one run or one goal. Many basketball games are won by one or two points. So, too, with golf tournaments, where one or two strokes may be all that separates the winner from the competitor who comes in second.

It's the same with risk. The company with the worst risk management style will still prevent some risk, and the company with the best risk management style still cannot prevent all possible forms of risk. It is the small difference—the middle third that Francesa referred to—that can make the difference.

Take baseball as an example. It has a long season, more than 160 games, and a lot of things can happen: a team can be "hot" or get "cold," a star player may be injured, the travel schedule may be tiring. Still, there are slightly more than fifty games in the "middle," between the one-third a given team will likely win if it is good and the one-third it will likely lose if it is bad. If the middle games are split evenly, each team stays in its relative position. If, however, a team wins an extra five or ten games in that middle portion, that may well make the difference between success and failure at the end of the season. Five additional wins out of fifty is one in ten; ten additional wins is one in five.

Small things do mean a lot.

In the early months of 2009, there was much media coverage of a peanut company based in Lynchburg, Virginia. The company had been linked to a salmonella outbreak that may have caused nine deaths and 637 illnesses. Scores of products, from peanut butter and crackers to dog food, had to be recalled. The government barred the company from certain contracts, law suits were filed, and, on February 14, 2009, *The Wall Street Journal* reported that the company had filed for bankruptcy. Was this a systemic breakdown of the company's control and safety systems or the actions of a single worker who failed to clean a food-processing machine properly? We do not know—these details have yet to emerge—but the message is clear. Big risk may come from small things.[11]

Returning to Coach Paterno, he makes the same point in a slightly different manner, when he said: "The will to win is important. The will to prepare is vital."

"Tone" is fine, but to be truly effective any presentation must be backed up with concrete action. Without such effort, it is merely the recitation of platitudes, and these do not have much staying power or positive effect. Think back to the description of the morning routine set forth in Chapter 1. All of it is designed to manage risk, but our actions are so ingrained that we do not consciously think about them much. They are the "little things," or, as Coach Paterno said, "the will to prepare."

TONE AT THE TOP

Always an important issue in the conduct of any corporation, especially after the Enron prosecutions and the 2002 Sarbanes-Oxley, or SOX, legislation, which stiffened requirements for financial transparency in public corporations, "tone at the top" became a sort of corporate mantra, as if repeating one's code of ethics often enough would somehow ward off evil spirits. (Both Enron and Bernie Madoff had very impressive statements of corporate ethics.) If one follows the issues of corporate governance and risk management, after a while you get tired of hearing the policies enunciated. That is not to say there is anything wrong with declaring them—it is good in its own right, but repetition of the mere words is not enough.

Two quotes may be useful in understanding the psychology involved. The first is from the noted writer Somerset Maugham, who once wrote: "She plunged into a sea of platitudes, and with the powerful breast stroke of a channel swimmer made her confident way towards the white cliffs of the obvious."

It is both fine and important for those at the top to express the proper and correct sentiments, but, by itself, this is not enough. Time, effort, and concrete action are required. But even more important is the need to live the creed, to do what you espouse. Many years ago, when I was a young Army officer at the Army Infantry School at Fort Benning, Georgia, the guiding principle was both simple and demanding—"leadership by example." It is expected and politically correct to "say" it—that is easy. It is another thing to do it.

The second quote illustrates this point. St. Francis of Assisi is reported to have once said the following: "Preach the Gospel. Use words if you must."

This very simple but powerful statement reminds us that our actions are more powerful than our pronouncements. At various points in my career, I had hundreds of people working for me. When you are a boss, you are a billboard visible to all. People watch and form judgments that are based on your actions. If your actions do not match your words, your words will always be suspect and will have little impact.

I saw this firsthand. What follows is a true story, somewhat dramatic, but it serves to illustrate an important point.

WHAT WE CAN LEARN FROM "DAVE"

During the last stage of my FBI career, I was a section chief in the Criminal Investigative Division (CID) at FBI Headquarters (FBIHQ). Among my responsibilities was running the Undercover and Sensitive Operations Unit (USOU). We reviewed and approved all criminal undercover operations (UCOs) proposed by the FBI's fifty-six field offices. When we got done reviewing them, they went to a committee of senior FBI and Department of Justice (DOJ) officials for further review. This process of repetitive review was our way of trying to limit risk.

Among the duties of USOU was the training of new undercover agents (UCAs). This was normally done in a two-week course at the FBI Academy at Quantico, Virginia. One of the great risks facing many UCAs is corruption; there is a lot of easy money flying around, and, for the weak of character, temptation may be great.

To bring reality to this training, especially on the issue of corruption, from time to time we hired a "flopped cop." This is an old police term for an officer who has been caught in an act of corruption and fired and/or prosecuted. The man we hired had once been a rising star in a major metropolitan police department. He had made the transition from patrolman to detective easily and was so highly regarded as a detective that he was hand-picked for a new and elite narcotics unit. The unit was well equipped, funded, and staffed and was the envy of most other detectives.

Anyone who has ever seen any of the *Dirty Harry* movies or other movies of that genre knows that the premise is simple and, to some degree, appealing—"The system doesn't work, so I have to take matters into my own hands." In the field of ethics, this is called "noble cause" corruption: "I know what I am doing is against the rules or the law, but I am justified in doing it, because my cause is noble." However romantic that may seem on the surface, it usually leads to results that are anything but noble. That is what happened to the detective in question.

Frustrated by the pace and requirements of the legal system, detectives assigned to the unit began to make narcotics arrests, usually seizing a fair amount of cash and drugs. Over time, they adopted their own system. They would throw the drugs down the sewer or into the river and keep the money, purportedly as a way of "punishing" the drug dealer. While they may have, in their own way, achieved their goal, they also kept the money. Things got worse. After a while, they not only kept the money but also kept the drugs. Eventually, the entire unit became involved, up to and including the bosses.

Finally, federal authorities got wind of the operation and nabbed one of detectives, whom I shall call "Dave." Dave was a bright guy and understood the justice system very well. He also realized that he was dealing with the "Feds" and that they could come down on him hard. Thus, he was induced to "wear a wire," a concealed body recorder, return to his unit (no one knew he had been arrested), and record the activities of his colleagues. He did this for well over a year and, meeting frequently with his federal handlers, handed over tapes and provided testimony to a grand jury. After a period of time, those conducting the investigation decided they had enough evidence on just about everyone to bring the thing down. Arrests were made, and the machinery of the federal justice system swung into action.

The results were not pretty. The police department in question fired everyone as quickly as their regulations and procedures permitted. Former police officers were arraigned and jailed and had to post hefty bail bonds to "make the street." As time wore on and the media continued to pound this story, several officers, faced with the reality of disgrace and the prospect of serious jail time, committed suicide. Eventually, the others were convicted, and most went to jail for substantial periods.

When we found Dave, he had served his time and was working here and there when he could even find work. The toll on him had been tremendous, a result not only of the tension of wearing a wire (he could have been killed had it been discovered) but also of the need to lead a double life as both a rogue cop and a reluctant "good guy" and the consequences that he saw befall his former colleagues, many of whom were his friends.

When we hired him, he would come to the FBI Academy for half a day and make a two- or three-hour presentation to the class. One of his most telling stories was this one:

I didn't become a cop to become a crook. I wanted to be a good cop. But I became a crook. But let me tell you something. In every organization, 5 percent of the people are straight—you can't tempt them to do wrong. And in every organization, 5 percent of the people are dirty—no matter what you do, they are going to be dirty. The other 90 percent are waiting to see what happens.

One may view Dave's statement as either poignant and insightful or as a cynical rationalization to explain why he was a "good" guy who just happened to fall in with the wrong crowd, but I think the statement does speak to a powerful truth. Tone at the top is fine, and necessary, but without action through both word and deed, without frequent and forceful repetition, without monitoring to ensure compliance and catch drift early, it may not mean as much as we would like to think it does.

There are several learning points in Dave's story. This was a large, sophisticated police department that was fully aware of the potential issues of corruption that can infect any organization, police departments included. Accordingly, it had controls in place. It monitored citizen and suspect complaints. It had an Internal Affairs unit staffed with veteran detectives who actively investigated possible violations of departmental regulations or the law. It scanned reports and statistics to see if any patterns were unusual and could possibly indicate some form of wrongdoing. Yet, it missed the downfall of not only an entire unit but an elite and well-publicized unit. Why?

Writing two millennia ago, the historian Juvenal made the following observation: "Custodiet ipsos Custodes?"(Who shall guard us from the guardians?). The police are supposed to be the guardians of the public (indeed, our term "police" comes from the Greek word "polis," which means "the people.") The rogue detectives changed from guardians to menace. Internal Affairs and other controls were supposed to detect or prevent that behavior, but it did not happen.

Lest we think that police departments and the Daves of the world are aberrations, please reflect for a moment and consider the following. There is a piece of folklore (or conventional wisdom, if you prefer) that at about age eighteen, when we leave the nest and those who raised us, we are fully equipped with a complete set of moral values. These are the values often bandied about by politicians—hard work, respect for others, love of family and country, fair play, and so on. It is as if nothing significant happens to us for the rest of our lives. I believe this is unrealistic, and I believe that, after reflection, you will come to the same conclusion.

Every organization of which we are a member for any period of time has the capacity to change us. Indeed, that may well be one of the organization's prime objectives. (Please note that I dedicate this book to three institutions that I believe shaped my life for the better.) This change can happen in ways both good and bad. The U.S. Marine Corps (USMC) is rightfully famous for its ability to take young people and turn them into patriotic warriors, willing to fight and sacrifice to protect their country and their fellow Marines. It has a long record of accomplishing this transformation. All military organizations, and indeed all organizations, do something similar, to some degree. If the objective is good, the end result will be fine. But, even if the organization, or at least elements of it, has begun to drift into unethical behavior, the process still operates. I think this is what Dave was trying to say—he thought he was a "good" cop, but he was unable (or unwilling) to resist the drift.

This brings us to the question of how we think about controls meant to assist us in detecting and preventing risk.

ATTENTIVENESS AND AWARENESS

Trent Gazzaway, managing partner of corporate governance for the professional services firm Grant Thornton LLP (GT), has been

helpful in more ways than one as I prepared this book. Not only did
he consent to an informative interview, but he also made available
early copies of documents produced by a highly respected professional team effort for which he served as project leader. This effort,
sponsored by the Committee of Sponsoring Organizations (COSO)
of the Treadway Commission, deals with how we should think about
and monitor our internal control systems and procedures.[12] The
three monographs are titled *Guidance on Monitoring Internal Control
Systems—Guidance*, *Guidance on Monitoring Internal Control Systems—Application*, and *Guidance on Monitoring Internal Control Systems—Examples*.

For those interested in how control systems operate to help manage risk, there are few better reference sources than these monographs. Control systems are like the smoke detectors now common
in most dwellings. It is fine to install them, and they give a height-
ened sense of security, but the wise person will change the batteries
and test them from time to time. So, too, with control systems.

As I noted in the Introduction, Tom Brokaw, speaking about
the financial meltdown that overtook the world in 2008 and 2009,
observed that those at the top simply did "not know what was going
on." The board and audit committee have to be alert to "drift." The
"C suite" executives, assuming they themselves are not drifting, have
to be alert to drift, and so on down the line. Such attentiveness and
awareness are the heart of risk management. While they are the
infrastructure of risk management, all of the tight control systems
and sophisticated IT systems spewing forth data may not pick up
the risk that comes from the human heart and mind, and this can
be the most dangerous risk of all.

A letter to the editor of *CFO* magazine commented upon the
credit risk issues brought to light by the subprime mortgage crisis of
2009. The writer noted that it is no longer enough to do the initial

due diligence quickly and tuck it away in a "credit file." There must be continuing monitoring of credit risk, as conditions change constantly.[13]

So, too, with risk and "drift."

NOTES

1. William G. Parrett, *The Sentinel CEO* (Hoboken, N.J.: Wiley, 2007), p. 1.
2. Ibid., pp. 8–11
3. Ibid., pp. 16–20.
4. Ibid., pp. 32–33.
5. Ibid., p. 34.
6. Ibid., p. 35–52.
7. Karl Albrecht, *The Northbound Train* (New York: AMACOM, 1994).
8. Ibid., pp. 68–71.
9. Kurt Reding et al., *Internal Auditing: Assurance and Consulting Services* (Altamonte Springs, Fla.: Institute of Internal Auditors Research Foundation, 2009), pp. 3-9–3-13.
10. Ibid., pp. 5–20.
11. Jane Zhang, "Peanut Corp. Files for Bankruptcy," *Wall Street Journal*, February 14, 2009, p. A-3.
12. *Guidance on Monitoring Internal Control Systems* (Durham, N.C.; American Institute of Certified Public Accountants, 2009).
13. Pam Frank, "At Risk," Letter to the Editor, *CFO* (February 2009), p. 12.

5.

· ·

WHY THINGS GO WRONG

· · · · · · · · · · · · · · · · · ·

This is the longest chapter in the book, but I think it may be the most instructive. It relates to the area where I spent a lot of my professional time and, perhaps, learned the most. Again, it is important to note that the discussion focuses on generic issues and pertains to all forms of risk. Risk occurs across all industry boundaries and in corporations of all sizes. While much of the material concentrates on fraud and related matters, it is hardly a narrative of everything I have seen in my career, much less all forms of corporate fraud and, therefore, forms of risk. (For those interested in learning more about corporate fraud in all its many forms, I can recommend no better book than *Occupational Fraud and Abuse* by Joseph T. Wells. More details about the book can be found in note 2 at the end of Chapter 2.)

CEO AND "C SUITE" BEHAVIOR

The great competitive race driver Mario Andretti is reported to have said: "If you are under control, you're just not going fast enough."

His observation may ring true if one is in the field of competitive motor sports, but it presents a continuing challenge to boards and audit committees when dealing with the behavior of the corporation's most senior executives. This is a complex issue to deal with in many ways. On the one hand, we want "C Suite" executives to be bright, energetic, innovative, and aggressive. That is how shareholder value is created and preserved. At the same time, these same attributes may lead them into overly aggressive business plans, excessive risk-taking, and, in some instances, fraudulent behavior. Knowing where to draw the line and having effective monitoring and evaluation processes in place can make the difference.

As my friend and colleague Dr. Sri Ramamoorti has noted from the field of social science research, we have a "criterion problem." The example he uses is three people having a discussion about politics. They all have their own views, but what is the criterion by which we should judge the merit of those views? Evaluating executive behavior is a bit like this: what standard do we use to determine when aggressive behavior passes a tipping point and becomes reckless?

In the previous chapter, the issue of "noble cause" corruption and the often corrosive effects it can produce were discussed. This kind of corruption is hardly unheard of in the "C suite." Bending the rules "just once" or failing to make timely and proper notifications, since to do so would slow things down, can lead to bigger and bigger problems. The operative concept here is the "slippery slope." Ethicists often cite the fact, recounted in the saying "The highway to hell is traveled in small steps," that one small issue may lead to another until they become one or more big issues.

An example from law enforcement is the patrolman who begins to accept a free cup of coffee every morning from a restaurant on his beat. It is not a big thing, and surely there is nothing wrong with something as small as a cup of coffee. Over time, the practice may grow to include getting a reduced price on meals and perhaps even free meals. There may follow the holiday card with a $50 bill tucked discreetly inside with a nice note to the effect of "Get something nice for the kids." Now, the patrolman feels a sense of friendship with the owners, and who does not want to help a friend? Delivery trucks have to deliver supplies to the restaurant on a regular basis and, due to congestion, must often double-park in violation of the law. The patrolman excuses them these infractions, since every body's got to make a living, and who can deal with the parking issues in the city anyway?

Later, if the restaurant has a liquor license, there may be an altercation between two customers. An arrest inside the establishment might bring problems from the alcohol control board and put a valuable license in jeopardy, so the arrest is made on the sidewalk, if an arrest is made at all. The patrolman may sternly warn the combatants to cut it out, go home, and never come in the establishment again.

Thus it goes, like a snowball rolling downhill. So, too, with the behavior of those in the "C suite."

THE FEAR OF "DEAL KILLERS"

I was once in a forensic and litigation support practice that had recently hired a talented and experienced due diligence data researcher away from another major firm. She was excellent at her job and could find any manner of public-source data online that would enable a client to better evaluate the suitability of a given business deal or opportunity. We thought such services would surely be highly valued in the marketplace and serve as a source of revenue to us. Accordingly, we went to a number of merger and acquisition (M&A) firms to explain and offer our services. At one of the first firms we called on, we met with a very senior person with whom I had a fairly solid prior relationship. Our presentation was well done and expertly polished, and we reeled off the many benefits we could offer, the timeliness of our response to the firm's needs, and the very competitive pricing we were prepared to offer.

When the presentation was over, we were politely thanked and told we would be hearing something in a day or two. Sure enough, a couple of days later I got a call from the executive with whom I had a relationship. The conversation went something like this: "Joe, we really appreciate you coming in, and it was great to meet Susan. It sounds like you guys have some good stuff there. But, I have discussed this with my partners, and we're going to hold off."

At this point I thought he felt pretty confident about whatever due diligence they were performing, and did not want to add what might be an unnecessary expense. His next sentence proved that assumption wrong: "If you guys found something bad, it could be a deal killer."

"Deal killer" were his exact words, and they have always stuck in my mind. I thought the whole purpose of doing due diligence was to try to find out if there was any bad news, but he and his associates saw the world from a different angle. They had worked hard to get their opportunities and had spent a lot of time and energy putting deals together. To some degree, they had fallen in love with the deal. Besides, if the deal went through, there was a big payday for them; if it did not, they got nothing. News that could be a "deal killer" was the last thing they wanted to hear.

One can easily move away from the world of M&A to almost

any other aspect of corporate behavior or business transaction and find the same mindset. It can be dangerous if you are concerned about risk. People are concerned about the amount of work and effort that might be lost and are fully aware of the metrics on which their compensation is based. Risk management is rarely among them. They are prepared to go forward on the assumption that most of the time, nothing bad happens. (There is an old folk saying about "throwing good money after bad." This can also be referred to as "sunk cost." It means that once we have invested, financially or psychologically, in a given position, we have a strong inclination to stay with that position.)

Joel Spolsky, himself a CEO, comments on this in an article in *INC.* magazine, noting not only his own experience when confronting salespeople who obviously must meet demanding performance metrics but also the work of Harvard Business School professor Robert Austin. Spolsky notes that Austin, in his book *Measuring and Managing Performance in Organizations*, argues that, when you try to measure people's performance, you need to take into account how they will react to the external performance standards. Austin opines that people will tend to find ways of achieving their metrics, even if it is at the expense of other important things you do not measure, such as morale and goodwill (or, in our case, risk management). Austin, Spolsky notes, goes even further, arguing that performance measures do not sometimes backfire; they always backfire.[1] Samuel Culbert, in *The Wall Street Journal*, goes even further: he suggests that we get rid of them altogether.[2]

A number of friends of mine have pursued careers in professional sports leagues after retiring from the FBI, usually in some sort of security role. Several of them are or have been the top security official in their league. One shared with me his tactics regarding "deal killers."

Athletes, especially the young and newly wealthy people coming into the leagues, face risk from gamblers, organized crime figures, shady businessmen, con artists, unethical agents, and pushers of banned substances. They are required to go through a multiday orientation program during which all these dangers are explained to them by people long familiar with such matters and how they are investigated. During these sessions, there are three attractive young women of various races who serve beverages and snacks during breaks to these self-confident young men. On the last afternoon of the orientation, each of the women (all are professional models and are paid for their participation) come forward to explain to all the new players how they got AIDS.

The point is dramatic and, one hopes, lasting. Some "deals"— whether it is the lucrative business deal or the enticing relationship— need to be "killed."

UNADDRESSED RISK CAN BECOME AN OLD FRIEND

Many times we recognize a risk and determine to do something to address it, but the press of daily business gets in the way, and then there is always the cost to consider. After a while, nothing bad seems to have happened and we begin to get used to living with it.

This kind of behavior can be a risk multiplier, since few risky things get better with age or cure themselves. A case in point: I once had a multibillion-dollar client that had purchased a much smaller company to fill out its business line. The acquired company had been headed by the same CEO for a number of years, but a risk was involved. My client could not mesh the financial reporting systems of the acquired company with its own system and resolved to address that issue. Time went on, however, and the issue never did get addressed. The temporary "fix," which eventually became permanent, was to have the administrative assistant to the president of the acquired company capture the company's financial information each month on a spreadsheet and then provide it to the parent company so it could be input into the parent company's system.

This seemed to work, but the parent company had no effective means of verifying the subsidiary's data, short of sending in an audit team to check the supporting documentation. On occasion, it did this, and the numbers generally were supportable. Again, over time, the parent became less and less inclined to tie up an already busy internal audit staff with what seemed like a tolerable, if imperfect, system. More than a decade went by without independent verification of the incoming financial data. Finally, a follow-up check was made, and the differences between the numbers reported and the numbers that could be supported was well into the seven-figure range. We were called in, and our team ascertained that the actual discrepancy was much greater. The situation had been going on for a long time, and greed and temptation had taken their toll. The subsidiary president would, when the monthly transmittal of data was due, make "pencil adjustments" to the numbers to be reported to corporate. His long-time and fiercely loyal assistant would dutifully record the numbers and pass them on.

At the time of our work, the subsidiary with the independent financial reporting system had been under the corporate umbrella for more than twenty years, and we determined that the differences between the figures in the two financial systems were much larger than believed. It is easy to let things slide.

There are two lessons to be learned from this situation:

1. If a control or risk problem is not dealt with in a timely manner, it almost never gets better, and it often gets worse.
2. If you ever encounter a spreadsheet used to move data be-

ance metrics were tragic. On May 25, 1979, American Airlines Flight 191 from Chicago to Los Angeles crashed shortly after take-off from O'Hare Airport when an engine tore away from the fuselage. All 271 people on board died, as did two people on the ground. Later investigation by the National Transportation Safety Board (NTSB) revealed that improper maintenance procedures were the most likely cause of the failure. The maintenance manual for the aircraft, a DC-10, required that a certain procedure be performed to remove an engine for periodic inspection. Maintenance personnel evidently believed they had found a short cut; they used a forklift to brace the engine while they removed it. Investigation after the accident concluded that the use of this unauthorized technique put undue strain on one of the bolts holding the engine to its mount, causing it to crack under the stress of takeoff, thereby causing the crash.

The investigation does not seem to have delved into the issue of performance metrics for aircraft maintenance personnel, but I am sure they had them. Aircraft sitting on the ground or in a hangar are not making money, so perhaps the maintenance personnel were tempted to try to do the job as quickly as possible in order to get the planes back into the air. They meant no harm, but they perhaps were influenced by their performance metrics.

I recommend that every audit start in human resources with a careful examination of performance and compensation plans. These can often explain a lot about the numbers you see when checking compliance with these standards in various parts of the corporation. Bad or skewed numbers can come from both "small" mistakes and intentional manipulation, but they are both at the root of many of the corporate scandals and failures we have seen. (See, for example, one of the many articles on the Madoff matter.)[3]

REMEMBER HOW YOUR CORPORATION GREW

Corporations increase in size in many ways, but one method that is fairly common is by acquisition. As in the example earlier in this chapter, where a subsidiary's financial systems do not tie into the acquiring corporation's, a number of problems can arise.

Following an acquisition, the emphasis is on integrating business operations and executing the business plan that drove the acquisition in the first place. Integrating control and reporting systems is almost always a low-priority issue and may never get done. Like all anomalies, these nonaligning systems can be a breeding ground for future problems.

I have had a number of engagements where this was the primary issue. In one instance, the client was a manufacturer of industrial equipment, with a number of sales offices in North America. When the corporation started operations, many years before, it had a mixture of both in-house (proprietary) sales offices and a network of independent dealers. Over time, the corporation's strategy was to buy up these independent distributors and eventually achieve a network of proprietary sales offices. This was done, but, after a few years, the corporation began to realize that it had a problem because of an assumption it had made. It had assumed that, once a distributorship had been purchased, normally with a cash payment to the owners and often with a continuing management contract as well, everyone would be on the same team. Not all the former distributorships saw it that way. They still maintained the old "arms-length" mentality of trying to get the best deal they could from corporate, which now came as sales and performance incentives, to maximize their profits. Accordingly, they consistently manipulated the data that they sent back to their supposed corporate "parent" in any number of ways. They could do this because they knew the system better than the corporation did.

As noted earlier, when things go wrong, they often go wrong in bunches, and this was the case with this client. Not only were games being played with corporate, but the sales personnel were playing games of their own, with the full knowledge and permission of the former distributor, now a district sales manager. They did this by exploiting the nature of the relationship they had had with the corporation when they were still independent distributors. Their technique was a bit complex in operation, but simple in theory—they were using the district sales office to run their own businesses.

It worked like this. Under the old independent distributor status, they could make a sale to a client, then negotiate with corporate on the price of building the piece of equipment in question. Under this system, they did not have to tell corporate the price or terms they had tentatively agreed to with the client. The difference was the profit for the distributor and the salesperson. For some reason, when the corporation began acquiring distributorships, it maintained this procedure.

What was happening, post-acquisition, was that the district sales managers and the sales personnel still saw themselves as independent and not as the "team members" corporate had assumed they would become, and they saw no reason why they should let all the money slip away. Accordingly, a number of them set up shell companies without corporate's knowledge. These shell companies were inserted in the sales process between corporate and the customer to hide the difference between the invoice sent out by corporate and the inflated price the customer was actually paying.

This was a somewhat complex scheme, so let us walk through it for ease of understanding: The way the system was supposed to work was as follows: the salesperson would make a sale, negotiate with corporate on a price to build the product, inform corporate of the sales price, and send an invoice to the customer. The customer would then send payment to corporate, and the product would be delivered to the customer. The sales office and the salesperson would then be credited with the sale, in the form of commissions and bonuses.

That is not how it worked in practice. In practice, it worked this way. Suppose that the salesperson makes a tentative sale to a client at a unit price of $130,000. He does so on behalf of the shell company. The customer is interested only in the product and the price and does not particularly care from whom he buys it. In this industry, there are a limited number of buyers and a limited number of salespeople, so in most instances they have known each other for years.

The salesperson then negotiates a production price with corporate and later reveals the sales price to be $110,000, which is considerably lower than the sales price to which the customer really agreed. Corporate begins production and prepares an invoice to be sent to the customer based on the price of $110,000.

The salesperson explains to corporate that this is a "special" customer, so he prefers to hand deliver the invoices in order to be able to answer any questions or concerns. Thus, corporate does not send the invoice for $110,000 directly to the customer, sending it instead to the salesperson at the sales office. The salesperson then prepares and sends to the customer an invoice on the shell company's letterhead for $130,000. The customer pays the shell company $130,000. The salesperson cuts a check to the sales office for $110,000 and keeps the $20,000 difference. Corporate receives funds for what it believes was the sales price of $110,000 via an intracompany transfer. The salesperson explains to corporate that this was a misplaced payment, as the customer mistakenly sent it to the sales office rather than directly to corporate.

This scheme worked for years and survived any number of audits. Upon investigation, it becomes clear that there are obvious questions that should have been asked along the way:

- ➤ Why did some salespeople have to hand deliver so many invoices, and why did these same salespeople seem to have so many misdirected payments?
- ➤ If the ultimate Customer was Company A, why were the invoices being paid by Company B?
- ➤ If the shell company was, in fact, a legitimate customer, why weren't they listed in business directories, why were their state public incorporation records murky as to their owner-ship, and why were they operating out of a post office box?
- ➤ Why was product being paid for by one company but being shipped to another?

The moral of the story is to look for patterns in corporate data. Keep an eye on the paperwork and the money. We got the invoice master file from corporate and ran it against the addresses of all salespeople and all sales offices. If we saw invoices being sent to the sales offices, that was a place to start looking. We also got the misdirected payment master file from corporate and looked for patterns by sales office and by salesperson. Why were some offices' payments so much higher than others? If you know what to look for, you can pick up such discrepancies and spot potential issues and risk.

An important point: the same techniques can be used to detect and identify almost any form of risk. We just need to be aware of them and willing to use them.

LOOK SIDEWAYS

Fraud or any other form of risk caused by human failure is not always fun to deal with. We have to question our own people, ask pointed questions, amass documentation, survey damage, and make tough decisions. Therefore, I have seen a tendency in many corporations not to want to look sideways. It is too easy and tempting to say the comforting buzzwords: "We had a bad apple," "Let's put this behind us," "Let's move on," "Let's write a rule and make sure this never happens again." All tempting and pleasant, like getting out of a dentist's chair, but in the long run it creates a form of risk in and of itself.

Two friends and colleagues, attorney Peter Anderson and psychiatrist Daven Morrison, came up with and refined a great term to describe situations such as this—"ABC." It refers to the question of whether you have a bad apple, a bad bushel, or a bad crop.

Corporate clients prefer to think that they have had only a bad apple and that there is no need to check the bushel or the crop. I can understand why. To do so prolongs the psychological anguish, takes time and money, and leaves the dread that something else will be found and will have to be dealt with. I am not advocating that one incident need cause a top-down review of everything, but at the same time I have seen more than one client have the same problem over and over and have to deal with it again because it did not look sideways the first time.

If executive A has found a way to manipulate data or commit fraud, is that person the only one doing so? If unit B is taking short cuts on maintenance procedures, is it the only one doing so? The irony is that once you have found out what happened in the initial incident, checking for it elsewhere is much easier, since you know what to look for.

This is what happened with the manufacturing company, discussed earlier, that acquired the distributorships. When we finished our work on the one location, we suggested it look sideways. Managers were skittish, concerned about time and cost. We explained that all the hard work had been done; we had all the corporate data captured electronically, and we knew what to look for (in this case invoices going to anyone other than the customer and a high percentage of misdirected payments). The client inquired about the time and cost. In light of the prior work done, we were able to say that the cost would be minimal and would take only about three hours of computer analysis time. The client told us to go ahead.

The company had twelve other offices that also had problems. Because of this finding, it pulled internal auditors in from around the country and had us come back for a day and a half to train these people on the scheme and how it operated and also about the other games the former distributors were playing with corporate financial data. The teams went out and documented our suspicions; on the basis of this information, the corporation redesigned its entire field commission structure.

It was probably something the company should have done years earlier, but at least it finally addressed the problem and made something positive out of what could have been perceived as only a "bad apple" situation.

NEVER TOTALLY TRUST A PIECE OF PAPER YOU DID NOT CREATE

It is likely that many of you have heard of the book and movie *Catch Me If You Can*, about the life and exploits of Frank Abagnale, a self-confessed counterfeiter as a young man, who turned to being an imposter to heighten the chances that the unwary will accept his checks. Since he went straight, he has compiled an impressive list of accomplishments as a legitimate citizen. He has a highly successful company and is a consultant to numerous financial institutions and corporations, a frequent speaker to law enforcement agencies, and a frequent lecturer at both the FBI Academy and FBI field offices.

In 2001, another one of his books came out. Titled *The Art of the Steal*, it recounts his career as a counterfeiter and also discusses the techniques he utilized to accomplish his deeds.[4] He takes the reader from the old days of White-out and razor blades up to the present when laser printers and computer scanning abound. The book is highly readable and compact in structure, yet imparts a lot of information. The more you read, the more wary you will tend to become. Those skilled in the uses of technology can counterfeit almost anything.

I learned this secondhand during the course of an engagement. I had a client in New Jersey that was a subsidiary of a holding company in Atlanta. The internal auditor of the parent corporation came to New Jersey to discuss the progress of the inquiry, and, over lunch, Abagnale's book came up. The auditor mentioned an interesting story about his experience as a student in one of Abagnale's classes:

> It was a typical Continuing Professional Education (CPE) class presented by Abagnale, with about forty students, held in a hotel conference room. If you have ever been to a CPE presentation, they tend to follow a similar format. You show up and check in, sign your name to a roster so you can receive your CPE credit, drop your business card into a bowl for a drawing that will be held at lunchtime, and grab some coffee and a danish.
>
> When the class starts, you have a seat with a temporary name tag in front of you. After an hour or two, there was a midmorning break, again with coffee and snacks. It lasted about fifteen or twenty minutes. What the students did not know, but would not have found

unusual, was that Abagnale was staying in that hotel. When the students filed back into their seats there, on the table in front of their seat, was a check, signed by them and on their company check stock, made out to Frank Abagnale.

Frank had all he needed. He had his computer equipment set up in his hotel room. He had their signatures from the sign-in sheet, and he had their business cards with the company logos on them from the drawing bowl. Doing some quick scanning, he was able to produce each in probably less than thirty seconds.

As the internal auditor recounted the experience, Abagnale, who had no intention of ever cashing the checks, did it to impress upon them how easy it is to produce a forged document on little notice if you know what you are doing and have some basic information available.

As managers of risk, we tend to put a lot of stock in supporting documentation—the various forms and documents that support what we see on a computer screen or printout. Perhaps, after Abagnale's presentation, we should not be so sure of what we are seeing, even if we can hold it in our hands. In my career, I have certainly seen my share of forged or altered documents, but computers have the capability to change the risk equation significantly.

THE FOUR HORSEMEN OF THE APOCALYPSE

My client this time was a good-size retail chain, and it had a problem. It believed that it could not find $2 million in cash, and so it asked us to investigate. What we found was not pretty. The Four Horsemen of the Apocalypse had been riding and had left devastation in their wake. The Horsemen were:

1. **Expansion**. The retail chain had been growing rapidly, too rapidly for control and risk management systems to keep up.

2. **Acquisition**. Much of the growth had been fueled by acquiring smaller competitors. In addition to handling the business and strategy issues created by expansion, the company now faced the additional task of trying to integrate the disparate risk and control systems of the new companies into its existing systems.

3. **Consolidation**. In an effort to try to capture economies of scale, the acquiring company had consolidated and relocated all its back office operations, including all the accounting and financial functions. Many old-time employees chose not to move, so there was a time lag as new jobs were posted, applicants interviewed and hired, and training took place. Even when these new people were brought on board, the company still had fewer people than before it went off on the acquisition spree. It expected miracles from the notion of economy of scale.

4. **Outside Consolidation.** The banks the company had dealt with for years were also taking turns buying each other and were facing problems as they integrated their own control and risk systems and back-office operations. To compound this, since the retail client had bought other competitors that were serviced by their own banks, these operations also had to be coordinated—even as the banks used by their competitors were themselves in a period of buying and being bought.

To use a technical term, it was a mess. Our first site visit to the new consolidated financial operations center was an education in and of itself. Untouched monthly bank reconciliations covered much of the floor in piles three and four feet high. A complete bank reconciliation had not been performed in almost two years.

When it was all over, we determined that the company could not account for more $5 million. How any auditor or risk manager, internal or external, was supposed to make sense of that chaotic an environment is beyond me. Once again, as noted earlier, background noise had created an inherently more risk-filled environment.

In football, the quarterback, the running backs, and the receivers normally get all the glory, and the guys in the trenches, the linemen, are often overlooked. So, too, with corporations; the deal-makers and high-flying CEOs and CFOs are the ones that make the covers of the magazines, while the back-office staff labors in obscurity. This may be the way of the world, but it creates a lot of risk. It is possible to put too much stress on any system, even a good one.

END-OF-PERIOD PROBLEMS

End-of-period (EOP) is as old an issue as there is in corporate accounting. This phrase refers to the time, at regular intervals, that the books are balanced and sales, revenues, and profits or losses are counted. Typically, these accounting measures are calculated every quarter and then again at the end of the fiscal year. EOPs tend to put a lot of pressure on everyone—management is watching, the board of directors is watching, the financial analysts are watching, the business press is watching, and the shareholders and investors are watching.

All of this attention puts the people responsible for producing sales and revenue under scrutiny. The issue of corporate financial performance is at stake, as are, in many cases, bonuses and incentives. There is both pressure and temptation. The issue of EOP "adjustments" is as old as accounting itself; there have been numerous instances of people yielding to temptation in reporting EOP financial results. Usually, if you know what to look for, you can pick up on the patterns of how they tinker with the numbers. These may include:

> **Extension of the Period**. Techniques include pulling sales made in the first few days of the next period back in the period in question.

> **Last-Minute Sales of Shipment**. Sent literally on the last day of the period, often a minute or two before midnight. These often have to be adjusted in the early part of the following period.

> **Overshipping or Shipping the Wrong Product**. This allows companies to "book" the sale and recognize the revenue, while handling customer complaints and returns in the next period.

> **Premature Renewal of "Evergreen" Contracts**. An "evergreen contract" is one in which a client has a standing order for goods and services, which the client can cancel or renew at the end of the contract's duration. Renewing "evergreen contracts" early even though the customer has yet to sign up for another year can boost revenue.

> **Revenue Management**. Some periods are better than others. If you have hit your objective for the period in question, there are techniques that enable you to "park" excess revenue so that it can be used in a subsequent period that might not be as successful. This is also referred to as "revenue smoothing."

> **Repeated Expansion or Extension of Credit Limits**. In effect, the company is funding people to buy its products. In some instances, this is called "channel stuffing."

Any experienced accountant, auditor, or forensic consultant can provide dozens of other examples, but EOP manipulation is always a potential issue.

BEWARE BAD BASELINES

This has nothing to do with baseball. It refers to the fact that you may have inherited or become accustomed to some bad numbers to the point that they no longer seem unusual.

I once worked with a company in which a payroll clerk had been stealing from the employer for more than fifteen years by putting one or two fictitious "ghost employees" on the books. (ACFE data indicate that the average occupational fraud goes on for eighteen months. Some, however, can last years.) The clerk had a mechanism for pocketing the money and probably would never have gotten caught had he not tripled the number of ghost employees over a fairly short time frame. This sudden jump in labor cost attracted the attention of the corporation, and an investigation was launched. Had the clerk maintained his normal level of theft, it might have gone undetected forever, since the corporation had assumed that its labor costs were "normal" because they were stable (if inflated).

ZERO-TOLERANCE PROGRAMS

I have dealt with zero-tolerance programs often, and they typically say something both profound and dramatic: We will tolerate no misconduct, and offenders will be dealt with severely. It sounds great and is not an unwise position to take, if you are willing to back it up. These programs have two major problems—uniform enforcement and the need for additional supporting resources—and they can be the source of much anguish.

I was once asked to review the new code of conduct for one of the package delivery companies. It was very well written and impressive, but it said something that caught my eye. It said, roughly, "Any violation of law will be grounds for immediate dismissal." Very impressive, but fatally flawed. I had seen this company's trucks in any number of major cities and had observed that, to make their deliveries anywhere near on time, they had to park in unauthorized areas and zones. It was not unusual for a single truck to pick up six or more parking tickets in a day. I mentioned this to the client. I do not know what it did with this sentence, but this kind of position can create problems, since there may be no realistic way to uniformly enforce it.

If a company adopts a zero-tolerance policy and fails to enforce it uniformly and to monitor it adequately, it leaves employees to guess what else the company is willing to tolerate. That is not a good situation.

The "uniformity" issue is often the topic of wrongful-discharge lawsuits. There is an all-too-human temptation to tailor sanctions to fit the nature and history of the employee. Thus, if a long-time employee who is a "nice guy" commits infraction A, that person may get a lighter penalty than an employee with less tenure who is unpopular. Such disparities give lawyers plenty to work with should the sanctioned employee decide to sue, because there is a difference between policy and practice—the rule book says one thing, but the corporation may have done another. Therein lies the risk.

So, too, with staffing issues. I once had another client with a zero-tolerance policy, and all possible violations were referred to internal audit. This function already was tasked with executing an annual audit plan and also had to deal with a swarm of potential zero-tolerance violations. Accordingly, the staff were flying around the world frequently and wearing themselves and the travel budget out. Their intentions were good, but under the circumstances they did not really have a chance to look at any particular allegation in depth. They were more likely to give each charge a quick look and then move on to the next one.

The moral of the story is this: Zero tolerance is fine, if you are prepared to uniformly enforce it and if you are willing to devote the resources to fully investigate possible violations. To do otherwise creates unintended risk, since employees are unsure of what exactly you mean and how serious you are about your message.

THE BOOK OF LOSERS

Many years ago, when I was an FBI new-agent trainee, one of our instructors held up the hefty FBI Manual of Rules and Regulations. Pointing to it, he said: "Folks, this is the book of losers. Every rule in here is because somebody screwed up. Try not to add to the book."

This was amusing, but it also highlights an all-too-common organizational tendency. When an organization has had a problem, it "solves" it by writing a rule. Over time, like junk in the garage or attic, the rules build up, often to the point that no one can obey all of them every day. Many times, they have not even heard of half of them, and of the ones they have heard of, a fair number may be outdated or so seldom become an issue that people come to forget them.

When employees are unsure which "rules" are in effect at any given time, they may tend to wander. They know that rule 5527 is rarely enforced, and 1399 is enforced only on occasion, and rule 2314 is never enforced, and so on. Being thus unsure of what the "real" rules are, they may make their own judgments and proceed accordingly.

I experienced this when I was drafted to be part of an FBI team to review all our internal regulations and manuals. The FBI is a thing of great precision, and every rule had a memorandum behind it to show why it was being proposed and who had approved it. We divided the rules in the manual into sections and sent them back to the units that had promulgated them. Even given the FBI's insistence on precision and accountability, when we were done, we could not find a home for fully 30 percent of the rules. Neither we nor anyone else knew where they had come from. They were just there and had been there for years.

In such a rule-intensive environment, employees tend to make their own judgments as to what is important and what is not and what management cares about and what is there for the sake of being there. This can create risk if they make a faulty judgment. Also, management can have a false sense of security because "we made a new rule to address this." Without adequate training, follow-up, and monitoring, the new rule may mean little and become lost in the sea of other rules. More risk can ensue.

After the Enron disaster, there was much fanfare and also anguish over passing the Sarbanes-Oxley legislation, which forever changed the corporate and accounting landscapes, put significant (and expensive) certification requirements in place, and restricted the manner in which accountants could interact with the firms they audited, among other provisions. For all the hoopla and cries of alarm about SOX, as it is known, the changes went into effect. Less than a decade later, there was another round of corporate and, this time, quasi-governmental (Freddie Mac and Fannie Mae) implosions.

I imagine that more than a few people reacted with shock and disbelief, shouting, "But we had a rule!"

Actually, they had a law, but people react to their performance metrics and, as people will do, their immediate self-interest. Many obeyed the new rules, but some sought ways around them, if not directly then indirectly, much as we might brush by another pedestrian on a crowded sidewalk.

Return, if you will, to the definition of fraud from *Black's Law Dictionary* set forth in Chapter 2: "All multifarious means which human ingenuity can devise. . . ." The actions that led to the economic meltdown of 2008 and 2009 did not have to be fraudulent; they could just be clever responses to a rule or a law. Human ingenuity is a powerful thing, and, like water flowing downhill, it will seek to find a way around obstacles.

Over the years, I have done a fair amount of teaching and enjoy the interaction with the students, most of whom are midcareer professionals. I also learn a lot. During the morning break at one presentation, a student who was an internal auditor approached me to discuss a scheme he had just heard about. There was a small company with only a couple of hundred employees whose owner was very tight on controls, to the point that he insisted on personally signing every check that went out, even payroll checks. The clerk who prepared these would dutifully present them each pay period but had, over time, developed a system. He put a "ghost employee" on the payroll but bumped the state and federal tax withholding so high that there was no net pay, therefore no check to sign. At the end of the year, he could file an income tax return in the name of the bogus employee and pocket the money. Human ingenuity strikes again.

Fraud happens. There are probably 40,000 certified fraud examiners (CFEs) in the United States alone, and that does not count attorneys and others who may not have joined the association. Why are there so many of us?

Because fraud happens.

LACK OF ATTENTION AND RESOURCES

Sometimes a corporation simply does not have the capability to investigate its own problems, much less anticipate and manage them.

Why this is so, I surmise, is that it assumes such events will not happen at all or at least will not happen that often. I have seen this often, in corporations great and small; indeed, it is the main reason I and my team get called in in the first place.

Although I am hardly a computer guru, I have great respect for what computer forensics can do. I must note, however, that there is a significant difference between computer forensics and mainstream corporate IT and MIS functions. The latter may have project-development responsibilities, but staff devote most of their time to keeping the system up and running and dealing with day-to-day glitches. That is fine, but I have rarely seen an IT/MIS function that had the time, training, mindset, or inclination to get involved with interrogating automated data systems, even the ones that it runs.

Many corporations, when dealing with a problem, pay a lot of outside consultants more than a fair amount of money to do this job for them and, believe me, we welcome the money, but it does not have to be this way. We never force our services down companies' throats; we ask if they can perform some pretty basic analytical comparisons, such as running the vendor master file against the employee master file (this is one of the basic first steps in looking for "ghost vendors," an employee also posing as a vendor). Well over 90 percent of the time we get one of two responses—a blank stare, since the company has no idea of what we are talking about, or a protestation that staff are way too busy to take on anything new.

Thus, we and many more like us make money doing routine tasks ourselves. Corporations can take responsibility for investigating automated data systems not only in a time of crisis ("We have a problem and have to find out what happened as quickly as possible") but also as part of an ongoing preventive program to monitor areas of risk within the corporation. Apparently, such frauds are either not often considered or, if they are, they are viewed as highly improbable and, therefore, a waste of time and money. That's how consultants make money.

Elsewhere in this book I referred to the phenomenon of "good—quick—cheap," and, while amusing, it does have meaning. Consider these two recent examples, which say it all:

The multinational professional services firm KPMG recently released a study of the current economic issues facing the United States and most of the world. Its title captures the message: "Lack of Stature and Resources for Risk Management Cited as Leading Contributors to Credit Crisis, KPMG Study Finds."[5]

Follow this, if you will, with a synopsis of an article by Jonathan Macey, a Yale Law professor and author of *Corporate Governance: Promises Made, Promises Broken*: "Corporate boards are often the last to see what's wrong."[6] When it come to the management of risk, resources, awareness, and management may all begin with different letters of the alphabet, but they all mean the same thing.

BEWARE THE IT MENTALITY

I will in no way denigrate IT/MIS professionals—I think they do a great job, at least insofar as they see and conceive of it. However, they can sometimes fall victim to a mindset that creeps into their thought processes. They deal with data, and they tend to dislike unruly data.

I once had an engagement that involved a huge leasing company. It bought stuff, then turned around and leased it. The deal it had with the manufacturers of the goods was that the company would buy merchandise at one price; then, after a certain number of years, assuming fair wear and tear, the manufacturer would buy it back at another price. (As it turned out, there was a scheme going on here that we detected but that is not germane to the point I am trying to make.)

One of the first things we asked our computer forensics folks to do was get a disbursements master file and do a stratification analysis on it (i.e., to rank the disbursements by some metric—amount, date, payee). Now, our computer forensics people were attuned to what we did, and we worked with them often. We thought—pardon the phrase—we had taught them to "think like a cop."

When I got the analysis back, I began to look through it; then I scrolled to the bottom line. This was a big company, and it made billions of dollars of purchases a year. I knew what that number was, but, when I compared it to the analysis, there was about $400 million missing. I asked the lead computer forensics manager about the apparent difference and he replied, simply: "There was some data that wouldn't fit, so we excluded it."

Now, to an old investigator, certain questions come to mind: Why were the data different? Is there any pattern to explain why they didn't fit? How long has this been going on? Are all the discrepancies coming from just one or two places?

We look for indications of what might be unusual and, therefore, suspect. A number of data professionals (even computer forensics folks), on the other hand, may look to smooth out data to produce a neater file. This can cause danger, because many of us rarely question the data we are presented for analysis.

An important subset of the IT issue is that many corporate data do not fit into neat "data piles." Ira Winkler, in his book *Corporate Espionage*, sets forth some often overlooked sources: formal documents, draft documents, working papers, scrap paper, internal e-mail correspondence, legal and regulatory filings, miscellaneous records (e.g., travel, vacations, calls), press and open-source data, formal meetings, informal meetings, and casual conversations.[7] All of these can contain harbingers of looming risk, or they can become proof of the corporation's "obvious" nonresponse to risk, should bad things happen.

MAKING INTELLIGENCE OUT OF DATA

I have earlier mentioned the role of background noise (inaccurate data) in impairing the ability of corporations to manage risk. There is yet another complicating factor that is even more insidious, only because it is so common and innocuous—information overload. As I have mentioned, I have had more than a few clients comment that they are "data rich and information poor." This is a common problem—how we take the multitude of data fed to us each day by the very smart machines we have built and make useful information, or "actionable intelligence," out of them? Dealing with data has become a job in and of itself. In his book *The Overflowing Brain*, Torkel Klingberg, a cognitive neuroscientist from Stockholm, discusses the neurological implications that these huge amounts of basically raw or semiprocessed data have for our physical ability to absorb and make sense of them.[8] He notes that the term "information overload" was coined by futurist Alvin Toffler back in the 1970s, when we thought we had a lot on our hands then. Seems like a quaint notion today.

We need not delve too deeply into the mysteries of the human brain to accept the conclusion that most days, whether it be our e-mails or our mail box, we seem to have more raw data than we can easily digest and likely more than we need. This Tower of Babel not only can be annoying; it can also mask risk. We try to cut through some of this clutter in Chapters 7 and 8, on organizational intelligence.

THREAT OVERLOAD

A subset, but an important subset, of data overload is threat over-load. I earlier referred to the response I got from harried "C suite" executives when trying to convince them of the value of the diagnostic and preventive services that the organizations I worked for felt highly qualified to offer: "If I listened to all you guys, I wouldn't get out of bed in the morning."

I can understand the feeling. Anyone who has spent any amount of time in law enforcement can relate to it. Threats, especially anonymous threats such as a telephone call or a note threatening an airline, building, governmental agency, or public space, are a fact of life, and there are more of them than you might suspect. Over the years, law enforcement has built up protocols for evaluating and responding to such threats. This is necessary, since it is not practical to shut down and evacuate each time a threat is received. For example, "A bomb is going off in the city today" does not give you much to work with, and, realistically, how do you shut down a city?

At the same time, as the events of 9/11 and Hurricane Katrina show, there is more than enough second-guessing and hindsight analysis to go around as to what could and should have been done once an event occurs. Executives in all sectors are put in a difficult situation. In retrospect, it appears that we perhaps overreacted to the Y2K scare (in case this has already faded from memory, it was the concern that computers would attempt to reset and stop functioning when the year 2000 arrived). Massive amounts of time and money were spent, and perhaps some of it made a difference, but by and large not much happened. Conversely, we now routinely see articles saluting those who predict crises, such as one in American .com, a publication of the American Enterprise Institute, that notes that Edward Gramich, a Federal Reserve governor and a professor at the University of Michigan, warned of the dangers of subprime lending ten years before it contributed heavily to a global financial crisis.[9]

What does an executive do but make a decision and hope things turn out all right? In light of the sometimes high volume of warnings received (which tends to look larger in retrospect than it does in the clutter of good news at the time the warnings are issued), evaluating threats appears to be a daunting and probably hopeless task. Actually, there are three things that greatly improve your chances of getting it right:

1. **Intelligence.** The more you know about your environment, the better equipped you are to make prudent decisions. We discuss this in detail in Chapter 6.
2. **Data Management.** By and large, threat evaluation is largely a matter of data management, if you take the time to do it and do it properly. In the example "A bomb is going off in the city today," would it not be useful to know that this is the seventh such call received in the past three weeks?
3. **Experience and Consultation.** These are actually two sides of the same coin, since consultation is nothing more than tapping into the experience of others, thereby ensuring that you have a greater reservoir of knowledge at your disposal.

I know the reaction. Like you, I have sat in more committee meetings than I care to think about, and we have all heard the funny quotes about committees. One of my favorites is from Sir Barnett Cook, a clerk in the House of Commons, who described committees thusly: "A cul-de-sac down which ideas are lured and then quietly strangled." But the bottom line remains—the more collective experience you can access, the better the decision.

MULTIPLE LOCKS ON THE FRONT DOOR

I have conducted a number of security vulnerability assessments, in conjunction with the IT folks, for a number of corporate data centers and have observed an interesting phenomenon. They often look like the bridge of a space ship from some science fiction movie. There are access controls, biometric readers, man-trap doors, photo identification checkpoints, and so on. It is all very impressive.

However, if you wait until about 8:30 P.M. and stroll through the building's offices and cubicles, then wander out back to the heavy metal trash dumpster, you can find all manner of sensitive information lying in open sight. Certainly, it is not as complete as what might come off a server, but it is there, nonetheless. We sometimes put seven locks on the front door and leave the back door wide open, thus creating a lopsided risk management environment that invites more risk, despite our best efforts. (Please refer to the discussion in Chapter 2 of the CERT-USSS 2004 study regarding insider risk, as an example.) We seem to be geared to defend our corporations against the seventeen year-old evil computer genius in some poor Eastern European country who in the middle of the night is going to hack into our computer systems and move a substantial amount of money to some remote country where it will be very difficult to trace and to find. That is a legitimate concern, but we often ignore or minimize the substantial amount of risk that resides within our corporate bodies (or in the careless handling of paper in cubicles or in the trash bin out back).

UNDERSTAND YOUR SYSTEMS

Since they are the conduits through which funds flow out of the corporation, payroll and disbursements are often the site of various problems. Two stories about payroll may be useful.

I had a client who used a vendor to provide payroll services, so each pay period an accounting clerk would input the payroll names and data and the vendor would do the rest. But one day the accounting clerk noticed an unusual feature of the system; it would accept a punctuation mark in the name field as a name. Thus, a period would suffice as a name. Before long, the clerk figured out a way to cut an extra check to himself each pay period.

Another payroll system I encountered was off-the-shelf. It not only accepted names and related data for checks but also cut the checks on company check stock (the check stock was supposed to be closely protected, but it was not). A feature of this system was that every time it began to run and print a series of checks, it would put a blank check, identical to a company check in every way, at the beginning and ending of every run. It did not take long for a few people to figure out what to do with the blank checks.

The point is that managers, and especially executives, don't know the quirks of various computer systems as well as the people who use them every day, no matter for what purpose. Therein can lie risk.

WE DO NOT PAY ATTENTION TO WORDS

I have a friend in New York who is the assistant manager of restaurants in a very upscale chain in midtown Manhattan. Let's call him "Springs."

He is a charming, friendly guy who knows the restaurant business cold, but he has a problem. He drinks. Not only does he drink, he drinks on the job. The supply is handy, and the liquor is free. He works from four in the afternoon until closing time, and by the end of the night he can be well into his cups. When he gets like this, he can become abusive to staff members he does not care for and has a tendency to mock and ridicule senior management. Eventually, this behavior got back to management. He was disciplined once, but allowed to stay at his highly lucrative location. When it happened again, he was transferred to another location in the chain where he would make less money. The manager of that location knew Springs's reputation well, and, while he valued his expertise in the restaurant business, he also knew his drinking could be a problem. Accordingly, on his first day there he laid down the law to Springs. "No drinking on the job."

Springs could be a charming and persuasive guy when he needed to be. He looked the manager square in the eye and mouthed this memorable line: "Boss, you won't catch me drinking."

"Catch" is the operative word here. He intended to keep drinking, but he would be more discreet about it and thus avoid further trouble.

Often, in dealing with risk issues, we receive assurances from people as to how things are going, how risk management systems are operating, and what kind of shape we are in.

Watch the words.

There are actually quite detailed theories and processes that claim to be able to spot deception in word usage. For an example, see the discussion of the use of critical content analysis and narrative discourse analysis in *Healthcare Fraud*, by Rebecca S. Busch.[10]

WHEN A GOLDEN APPLE DROPS IN YOUR LAP, CATCH IT

As an independent consultant, I have the opportunity to become involved in a number of interesting projects. One was to work as a subcontractor to a major professional services firm that had just landed a significant contract to review the operations of a large data center. The center in question had a ton of problems: it had thousands of clients to serve each day on very short notice (it tried to turn around clients' inquiries in no more than twenty minutes); it had more than a dozen stand-alone data sources it had to search; each data source had its own protocols and procedures; the data source systems were slow and balky, and many data searches had to be restarted because analysts did not follow the procedure the system demanded or their work took so long that the data system they were interrogating timed them out; the training program for analysts took six months, and even then it took two years on the job for analysts to become proficient at using the systems they had to check; the pay was low and promotional opportunities were limited; it took almost eighteen months to find, qualify, and hire a new analyst; and there were other, more lucrative, and less demanding jobs available nearby. In short, the company had a bunch of problems.

As part of the project team, I made a visit to the client site with several of the contractor's professionals, mainly IT people who were highly skilled in systems architecture and systems integration. I also often participated in follow-up conference calls following the team's site visits, when it normally dealt with the data center's IT people. Following one such visit, the team had a call-back to the client IT personnel to discuss its preliminary findings, and I was asked to participate.

When bidding on this work, the firm I was working for had come up with a budget based on a work plan, which in turn was based on certain analytical procedures it intended to follow. The contractor's IT folks executed this work plan to perfection.

During the call, the two client IT people with whom the team had spent a fair amount of time the week before were on the phone to provide additional information and to comment on the preliminary findings of the IT consultants. The conversation went something like this:

> "Hey, Ben and Jim, it's Jerry and Carl from XYZ Consulting, and we just wanted to follow up on a few issues from our visit last week. We also have Joe on the line."
>
> Ben: "Sure, what do you want to cover?"
>
> Jerry: "Well, we have issues A, B, and C we'd like to discuss."
>
> Ben: "OK, but that's not what's really going on here."

To an old investigator, this is a moment you live for; someone wants to tell you what is really going on. Since we were all on our computers during the call, I sent this e-mail to my colleagues from the consulting firm: "We really need to pursue the 'what's going on' comment." I got back a terse, "Let's see."

The consultants proceeded to run through their checklist and got much good information on what they thought the issues were at the data center, but they did not follow up on what the center's personnel thought the real issues were. Thus, a golden opportunity to perhaps get at the heart of the risk issues was lost.

Checklists are fine and useful, but they can blind us to much useful information if we become captives to them.

A case from the FBI illustrates this point. It became one of the largest spy cases in U.S. history, and it started with a drunken phone call. It is often referred to as the John Walker Family Spy Ring. The "ring" comes from the fact that, over time, Walker involved both his brother and his son in his activities. Walker was a U.S. Navy career enlisted man who served long stretches in cryptographic activities, where he had access to highly classified information. He considered himself a dashing, man-of-the-world type and sought to fulfill that image by selling U.S. secrets to the Soviet Union.

Even though I am a retired FBI special agent and senior executive, let me make it clear that I did not work on this case, have not talked to anyone who did, and have had no access to FBI files on it. All of my information comes from numerous news reports, books, and at least one made-for-TV movie about Walker. At the same time, I am aware of no public source information that contradicts the basic facts of how the case was developed. I use the case to reinforce the "golden apple" theory.

Walker's wife was, in many ways, a desperate woman. She had suspicions about her husband's sudden wealth, his new lifestyle, which included the purchase of expensive toys (including an airplane), and his penchant for cavorting with other women. Walker evidently saw himself as a "James Bond" type and lived his fantasy to the fullest.

The FBI has a headquarters in Washington, D.C., and fifty-six field offices (FOs) around the country. Each FO normally has one or more suboffices, called resident agencies (RAs), within the geographic region it covers. These may have from two to more than a dozen special agents (SAs) assigned to them, but while they are on such an assignment it is common within the FBI to refer to these people as RAs (resident agents).

Evidently, Walker's wife, drinking to ease her tension and pain, picked up the phone one night and called a resident agency. She got a resident agent who, although it was past the end of the normal workday, was still in the office. She began to recount her tale of woe, although her presentation was seriously affected by the state she was in.

In the FBI, as in all of law enforcement, you learn to deal with what are called "nut calls," and there are many funny stories about off-center or drunken citizens who decide they have something important to report, maybe a death ray beamed into their bodies or a

Martian in their backyard. It comes with the territory, and you deal with them.

When this agent got this call, he could have dismissed it in about thirty seconds, hung up the phone, and gone home. But he took the time to listen a bit and began to pick up some elements that rang true. He stayed on the line and developed, as best he could under the circumstances, information that could be verified: whether Walker was in the Navy; how long he had been there; what sorts of jobs he had held; where he was stationed now; what he was doing; who he was doing it with; what sort of money he was spending and what he was spending it on; what sort of car he drove, and what state it was registered in; whether she would be available to speak again in a discreet setting; and so on.

These are the sorts of questions any experienced investigator would ask, but the real key to the story is that the RA took the time to assess what was being told to him. Thus was the Walker spy case broken. And thus did the IT consultants perhaps miss a golden opportunity.

We inherit or prolong much risk when we fail to catch the golden apples that drop every now and then from the tree. Certainly, it takes skill, judgment, and experience to differentiate them from the apples that are merely rotten and dropping to the ground, but if we can, we may be able to eliminate an awful lot of risk.

There is another significant element to be gleaned from the Walker story. This tracks the insightful comments made in Chapter 3 by Trent Gazzaway. Walkers's wife did not call the director of the FBI with this important information; she called the first FBI number she could find in the local phone book, which turned out to be an RA in a small town somewhere in New England. People do not always disclose information to the "appropriate authorities," be they governmental or corporate. If so inclined, they disclose it to the first person or entity they can find that seems, to them, to make sense. Thus, we would be wise to remember Trent's observation that, to some degree or another, risk management is everyone's responsibility.

We discuss how to better achieve this ability in Chapters 7 and 8, on organizational intelligence.

IF YOU DECIDE TO JUMP, TRY NOT TO LAND ON A CONCLUSION

In Chapter 3, "Fast Eddie" Gartner recounted his injunction to the young automotive service technicians he trained over the years: "Clear your mind."

We are all rightfully proud of our education, training, and experience, and we take pleasure in being able to figure out what is happening more quickly than anyone else. This is good, in that it saves time (and also makes us look special in the process), but it can also pose a significant danger. If we do not listen enough and take prudent steps to analyze and verify, we may jump too soon, and we may land on the wrong conclusion. We may then find ourselves not only ignoring the real problem but wasting time, money, and effort trying to "fix" the wrong thing.

We may tend to do this because of the specialized perspectives we all have developed and instinctively carry with us as part of our psychological makeup. Consider looking at a house: as a former law enforcement officer, I may see the potential security vulnerabilities, an architect may see issues of style, and a landscaper may see issues with how shrubs and plants are utilized. We tend to view whatever we are look at from the perspective of our training and experience. One of the best explications of this was a book written by Harvard professor Graham Alison about the Cuban Missile Crisis, wherein he talks about what he calls "organizational routine." By this he refers to this same tendency. During a time of severe national crisis the military tended to propose a military "solution," the diplomats a solution based on statecraft, and so forth. Each specialty saw the issue from its particular perspective. The success of the Kennedy administration was in crafting a solution that used elements of all the potentially important resources.[11]

The tendency to view the world this way is all too human, even among top professionals. An article in *AARP* magazine reported that about 15 percent of all patients are misdiagnosed by medical personnel, with the result that about half of them suffer serious physical harm and perhaps even death. Certainly, medical personnel take into account a number of things in formulating a diagnosis: laboratory tests, physical examinations, and patient interviews. However, the article goes on to cite studies that indicate that most physicians interrupt a patient's description of her symptoms after eighteen seconds.[12]

Do they jump to a conclusion? Perhaps. Those interested in risk management would be well advised to be alert to the same all-too-human tendency in their own process of diagnosing the possible cause of, and solution to, risk. Interestingly, a recent study indicates that even medical personnel, such as radiologists, who study diagnostic tests but rarely meet a patient in person, have improved their diagnostic rates just by having a physical or digital photograph of the patient available when they do their analysis.[13]

FALSE POSITIVES

As was noted with regard to zero-tolerance programs, sometimes a corporate compliance or risk management program can be too aggressive or too sensitive to every ripple on the pond. This can not only burn out resources but also create a false sense of alarm. If everything is a crisis, sooner or later nothing becomes a crisis. In such an environment, a real crisis may get lost in the crowd.

There are a number of good, well-intentioned programs and tools in the marketplace that usually operate under some "red flag" banner—they have a program or technique that will measure risk and promptly alert you to it. Experienced risk professionals, especially the fraud professionals I know well, tend to take these systems with a grain of salt. Not that they are not good, but they are almost too good, as they tend to throw off a lot of false positives. Almost any hard-charging CEO would tend to show up as a potential risk under such a rating/ranking system. Some may, in fact, be problems, but most are not. Therein lies the issue. It is difficult to apply a formula to human behavior, especially that of powerful people in a dynamic corporate environment.

There are other analytic tools that also try to measure exceptions, such as those that examine the patterns in which numbers appear in, say, disbursement files (Bendford Analysis), but one must be alert for false positives here, too. Tools such as computer-assisted audit techniques (CAAT) can be helpful, but it is difficult to take the role of the experienced auditor or forensic consultant out of the equation.

There is a tendency to seek out "plug and play" solutions, since, although many of them are expensive, they appear to offer a "quick fix" that substantially reduces the number of people needed to manage risk. I understand the temptation, but it reminds me of an old FBI story that is supposedly true.

A young agent attorney had been assigned to the Legal Counsel Division at FBI headquarters. One day, a high-ranking executive came charging into his office and handed him an assignment that was critical, had to be done perfectly, and was due in two days. The executive also informed him that everyone was busy, so he could expect no help. As the story goes, the young agent replied: "You can have it good, quick, and cheap. Pick two."

If this is in fact a true story, that was one brave young agent, but his logic was sound:

IF	WILL NOT BE
Good + Quick	Cheap
Good + Cheap	Quick
Cheap + Quick	Good

Unfortunately, I am aware of no magic bullet that can handle management risk and that is good, quick, and cheap (although there are some fairly simple steps we can take that come close; we discuss these in Chapters 7 and 8).

LISTEN—AND LOOK

From time to time there is a flurry of interest in the use of "body language" to detect deceit or other human emotions and motives. Often, it seems, when a sensational and long-running criminal trial is on television every night, one expert or another will opine on what is "really" going on. Treat these presentations as you will, but there is much we can learn from not only listening but also looking. It does not happen all the time. In an age of e-mail and attached files, we have much less face-to-face interaction than we used to, but looking every now and then can yield benefits. (It has been reported, for example, that people who use e-mail to communicate are 50 percent more likely to lie and to feel justified in doing so than those who communicate by hard copy.)[14]

Here is one example. Many years ago, in New York City, there was a famous case involving an attractive divorcee who worked as a cocktail waitress. Over time, she struck up a friendship with one of her customers, a middle-aged, married businessman. The friendship turned into a romance, and they decided he would get a divorce and they would start over. The issue was that she had two kids from her previous marriage, and the kids did not fit into their plans. One day the kids disappeared, and she dutifully reported this terrible tragedy to the police.

Even though this was decades before the current emphasis on child abduction and abuse issues, the story got a lot of attention, and the police worked on it a lot. Then, one day, the children's bodies were found. The police made the painful call to inform the woman that they had some bad news and to ask her to come down to the local precinct to hear it firsthand. She did.

Like any grieving mother, she showed up with her defense attorney. In the eyes of veteran detectives, this was a flashing sign, and she went from being a victim to a suspect. She and her lover were later convicted of killing the kids.

The point of this story is that while data and information are important, behavior means a lot. Her behavior did not "fit."

I saw similar behavior many times in less serious circumstances, but one in particular comes to mind. The firm I worked for had been retained by the board of directors of a major charity after two disgruntled former employees told a reporter that the charity had falsified its numbers for many years to gain increased government funding. A major "exposé" followed, and the board, made up of successful and prominent professionals and businesspeople, was horrified. It wanted us to get to the bottom of the allegations as quickly as possible, as the charges reflected on the effectiveness of their oversight. As an afterthought, the board also asked us to be alert to a nagging suspicion it had that the CEO of the charity, who had held that position for three or four years, was more of a figure-head than an executive.

I was working with a senior audit partner named George, whom I had worked with many times and for whom I had the highest respect because of his knowledge of audit and accounting issues and his attention to detail. We called the CEO and scheduled a meeting for the following day. The meeting went well—the CEO was well groomed, intelligent, charming, and cooperative. As we wrapped up our interview, we asked him if we could next talk to his CFO. He had expected this and readily agreed. He fished a company directory out of his desk drawer and called the four-digit extension to advise the CFO that we would like to meet with him and would arrive shortly.

When we left the CEO's office, I stopped George in the hallway and asked, "Did you see that?"

"See what?" he replied.

"George," I said, "we just answered one question. What CEO doesn't know his CFO's office extension?"

The CEO was not only a figurehead; he was nonexistent for all intents and purposes and really had no idea of what was going on in the charity he was supposed to be running.

Looking can tell you a lot.

LOOK AT THE BASICS

I have rarely seen a risk issue that was sophisticated or exotic. Often, they boil down to basic principles. Two of the more common are failure to segregate duties and inadequacy of internal audit.

The principle of *segregation of duties*, particularly where money is involved, is as old as accounting itself, but it is still often violated. People share passwords, the person who writes the checks also does the bank reconciliations, salespeople enter their own orders, the person who does purchasing also does receiving, and so on. Violation of this principle is probably one of the most common causes of fraud risk, and it happens because people are busy or lazy or the corporation is looking to save money on personnel. Whatever the cause, it creates substantial risk.

Internal audit is the second line of defense after direct supervision, but it is often a weak line (there is more on this in Chapter 2). Generally, internal audit staffs are overworked, have poor promotional opportunities, have to travel a lot, perform work that sometimes puts them into confrontation with their fellow employees, have an annual audit plan that allows little time for the in-depth exploration of potential problems, get limited analytical support from IT/MIS, and are untrained in the detection of fraud and other forms of risk. In addition, many corporations use internal audit as a management development assignment, which means staff are rarely in place long enough to develop much hands-on experience.

Over the years, I have been part of training teams that provided instruction to both external and internal audit staffs. I always try to emphasize one thing: you do not have to "beat" an audit; all you have to do is outlast it. As noted, audit plans, internal or external, are things of complexity and timing. It is expected that a certain amount of work will get done in a certain number of areas in a certain amount of time. Disruptions are not welcome. This by no means is meant to say that an auditor will overlook something unusual, but he may be forced to work with old data, disorganized data, incomplete data, and so on. The auditor will certainly note such areas as something to be revisited next time, but next time could be a year or more away.

Of the hundreds of corporate frauds and problems I have been involved with, I rarely saw one that had not been through at least one audit, and often they had been through many, both internal and external. Remember the ACFE data—the average offender has been with the organization between ten and fifteen years. He has been through multiple audits and knows what gets looked at and how to deal with young auditors. To a large degree, they know the "system" better than the auditors. Problems persist, undetected.

This, in my experience, is the number one reason we are surprised by risk-related events, be they fraud, regulatory lapses, financial reversals, competitive challenges, or any of hundreds of other risk-related developments.

THE WINDOW

Over the past fifteen or so years I have given more than 100 classes and presentations. During this period, I have given a certain "test" to about 3,750 people, including CEOs, CFOs, attorneys, accounting professors, internal auditors, CPAs, lenders, students, and others. To date, three have gotten it right. For what it is worth, all three were young, and two were women.

The test is simple, and it is not a trick question. It goes as follows: You have a window that measures twelve inches by twelve inches. Your task is to increase the surface area of the window without making it any taller or any wider. The test is two dimensional. You may not bow the window in or out.

As readers, you have a distinct advantage over those in my classes and presentations, because you have more time to think. For a simple reason, to be revealed at the end of this chapter, I do not think it will make much difference. Some, but not much.

In giving this test, I normally allow the participants a minute or two to solve the question, but, realistically they are dead in the water in the first few seconds, so the additional time does not help much. When the time is up, I provide the answer and then ask a consolation question to award a prize I always give—a FBI baseball hat. I had to go to the consolation prize strategy because I got tired of hauling hats back from events. It was easier just to give them away.

The answer to the question appears at the end of this chapter, along with an explanation of why I use it.

IN CONCLUSION

I realize that this is a long chapter, but each and every one of the issues noted has caused risk that I have been called on to deal with at one time or another. We may be tempted to say that all of this is too much to try to address, that the cost is too high, that addressing such matters will get in the way of operations and limit profitability.

That may all be true, but the consequence is that we are living with a risk equation that is weighted toward the risk side.

SOLUTION TO THE WINDOW TEST

As the illustration shows, a window may measure twelve by twelve inches and come in many shapes. The mistake well-educated, intelligent people make is to assume that the window is square. They do this because many windows are square. But not all of them are. There is an old saying to the effect that "A dime held close enough to the eye can obscure the world." So can an assumption. If you assume a window is square and that it measures twelve by twelve inches, then its surface area is 144 square inches. Its surface area

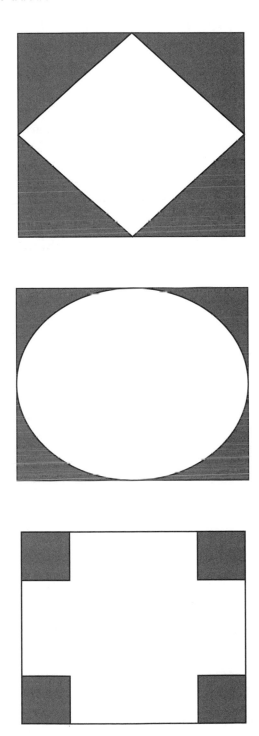

cannot be increased. However, if it is not square (see the dark areas in the illustrations), you can increase its surface area and still keep it twelve by twelve.

My point is that we make assumptions. Many windows are square, but not all of them are. So, too, with trusting people and accepting numbers as accurate. Most of the time our assumptions are correct—but not all the time.

Assumptions are tricky things. We could not live a normal life without them. When we go to bed at night, we assume that the house will not burn down and that the alarm will go off; we assume no one will steal our car overnight and that it will start; we assume that traffic lights will work properly and that the bridge has not collapsed or been washed out. At the same time, other assumptions can blind us to risk:

> ➤ We assume we have identified all our risk—but we have probably missed some.
> ➤ We assume the data being fed into our risk-monitoring systems is accurate—but not all of it is (think back to the property-casualty company).
> ➤ We assume our people are honest and conscientious—but not all are.

The French philosopher Paul Valery once commented that "A poorly observed fact is more treacherous than a faulty train of reasoning."[15]

There is much merit in that observation.

Each risk assumption carries with it a risk of its own. We cannot, in any reasonable sense, challenge our assumptions about all risk every day—we would do nothing else. At the same time, we might well benefit from challenging some every now and then. To refer to the comment, presented in Chapter 4, by sportscaster Mike Francesa about who comes out ahead at the end of a baseball season, the team that wins a few more of the middle-third games is usually the winner in the end.

NOTES

1. Joel Spolsky, "Employees Will Always Game Incentive Plans—Because the Geniuses Who Design Them Don't Anticipate How Employees Will Respond," *Inc.* (October 2008), p. 85.
2. Samuel A. Culbert, "Get Rid of the Performance Review," *Wall Street Journal*, October 20, 2008, p. R-4.
3. Aaron Lucchetti, Dionne Searcey, and Amir Efrati, "Madoff Probe Said to Find Fake Data," *Wall Street Journal*, December 17, 2008, p. A-1.
4. Frank W. Abagnale, *The Art of the Steal: How to Protect Yourself and Your Business from Fraud, America's #1 Crime* (New York: Broadway Books, 2001).
5. "Lack of Stature and Resources for Risk Management Cited as Leading Contributors to Credit Crisis, KPMG Study Finds," KPMG press release (January 6, 2009).
6. Jonathan Macey, "Holding CEO's Accountable," *Wall Street Journal*, December 9, 2008, p. A-15.
7. Ira Winkler, *Corporate Espionage* (Rocklin, CA: Prima, 1997), pp. 4–11.
8. Christopher F. Chabris, "You Have Too Much Mail," *Wall Street Journal*, December 15, 2008, p. A-17.
9. Thomas J. Healey and Matthew A. Scogin, "Data Detectives Are Making Financial Markets Safer and Better for Investors," American.com, November 17, 2008.
10. Rebecca S. Busch, *Healthcare Fraud: Auditing and Detection Guide* (New York: Wiley, 2007), pp. 207–238.
11. Graham T. Allison, *Essence of Decision* (New York: Little, Brown, 1971).
12. Jerome Groopman, "Why Doctors Make Mistakes," *AARP* (September–October 2008), p. 40.
13. Kevin Helliker, "Face Time: The Benefits of Seeing Patients as People," *Wall Street Journal*, December 2, 2008, p. B-9.
14. Anne Fisher, "E-Mail Is for Liars," *Fortune* (November 24, 2008), p. 57.
15. John W. Collins, *The Seven Fatal Management Mistakes* (Boca Raton, Fla.: St. Lucie Press, 1998), p. 101.

6.

· ·

HOW RISK IS DISCOVERED

· · · · · · · · · · · · · · · · · · · ·

Corporations use controls to try to manage risk. Generally, they seek to accomplish five goals. In *Cutting Edge Internal Auditing*, Jeffrey Ridley, citing prior sources, identifies these goals as:

1. Maintenance of reliability and integrity of information
2. Compliance with policies, plans, procedures, law, and regulations
3. Safeguarding assets
4. Economical and efficient use of resources
5. Accomplishment of established objectives and goals for operations or programs[1]

Kurt Reding and colleagues, in *Internal Auditing: Assurance and Consulting Services*, set forth thoughts and definitions on five major categories of risk control activities in corporations:

1. **Complementary Control Activities**. These are activities that, while not sufficient in and of themselves to mitigate a risk, can, when used in conjunction with other control activities, improve the risk mitigation environment.

2. **Detective Controls.** These activities are designed to detect unfavorable issues that may have arisen despite the presence of other risk mitigation control systems.

3. **Preventive Controls.** These are controls meant to deter the occurrence of unintended events with regard to risk issues.

4. **Directive Controls.** These are controls that provide guidance to help the company increase the probability of achieving a desirable outcome.

5. **Corrective Controls.** These are controls meant to address issues that may have arisen with regard to risk mitigation.[2]

In this chapter we focus on two of these sets of control systems—preventive and detective. Actually, these are two sides of the same coin, as preventive controls are meant to prevent bad things from happening, and detective controls are meant to pick up on unwanted occurrences as soon as possible.

Again, we return to an old and reliable source, the Association of Certified Fraud Examiners. ACFE has complied and published *Report to the Nation* since 1996, and it is a wealth of information for anyone interested in risk management, especially fraud risk, but again I must note that a great deal of what goes on with regard to fraud risk applies to almost all other forms of risk, as well.

The *2009 Report to the Nation* is available free and online at the ACFE website. The latest edition reviews, compiles, and displays the results of 959 corporate fraud events that were investigated and resolved during the period January 2006–February 2008. While the *Report* provides much useful data on many facets of fraud, let us turn our attention to those sections that pertain to the specific issue of risk detection.

As noted, corporations have a variety of controls systems available to them. The issue is how well these systems work, in this case with regard to fraud risk. There is a presumption to be made here, one with which you may or may not agree, but from my experience I think it is sound. The proposition is that fraud risk, about which we have fairly good firsthand data, is to a large degree representative of all forms of corporate risk, at least with regard to how it occurs and how it is discovered. If this is at least to some degree true, we can learn a bit from the fraud professionals who report their data and experiences in great detail to ACFE.

A small sample of findings from the Executive Summary portion of the *2009 Report* may shed some light on possible issues:

➤ Fraud schemes have a fairly lengthy life span, lasting almost two years before they are discovered.

➤ Corruption, which by definition requires the interaction of two or more people, is the most common form of fraud, accounting for 27 percent of all incidents.

➤ Perhaps most concerning from a control perspective is that frauds are much more likely to be discovered by a tip than by controls, audits, or any other means. Forty-six percent of the frauds discovered, investigated, and resolved during the time frame in question were discovered in this manner, despite the systematic, expensive, sophisticated, and overlapping control and risk-monitoring mechanisms in place. This trend was also found in data compiled from the *Reports* for the years 2002, 2004, and 2006, so it does not appear to be a one-time phenomenon.

➤   At the same time, controls do seem to have some impact, especially if carefully implemented, adequately staffed, and aggressively executed. ACFE reports that implementation of such controls appears to have a measurable impact upon fraud losses. A total of fifteen individual controls mechanisms were examined, and in every industry, whether categorized by industry type or corporate size, the existence of controls resulted in lower fraud losses. For example, corporations that conducted surprise audits suffered median losses of $70,000, whereas corporations that did not utilize this technique had median losses of $207,000. Similar results were found for corporations that had anonymous fraud hotlines (as discussed in much more detail in the chapters on organizational intelligence, there are both good ways and poor ways to utilize hotlines, as useful as they may be in theory); offered employee support programs; provided fraud training for managers; and had internal audit or fraud examination departments.

➤   Lack of such internal controls was the most common reason cited by forensic investigators for the occurrence of fraud events and losses. Lack of such controls was cited by 35 percent of responding fraud investigators as the primary reason such events occurred, and lack of sufficient management oversight was cited in 17 percent of the incidents.

➤   The *Report* advises that in 78 percent of the incidents, the victim corporations modified or enhanced their antifraud controls after the incident was discovered, investigated, and resolved. In 56 percent of the cases, the primary response was that management conducted a review of internal controls. Thus, it seems the most effective teacher in many situations is loss and bitter experience. (To quote an old Belgian proverb, "Experience is the comb that Nature gives us after we are bald." To use another analogy, I often say that when I got involved in the risk management field, I wanted to be a house painter—to work with clients to enhance their internal risk management controls and thus improve their risk prevention and detection environments. Now, after many years of experience and failure, I describe myself as a fireman. When the corporate house is on fire I, or someone very much like me, gets a call to come put it out. That seems to be what these corporate victims did, time and again.)

➢   Fraud, and perhaps most risk management lapses or misdeeds, is committed by first-time offenders. The *Report* noted that only 7 percent of persons involved in such activities had a prior conviction for fraud-related activities, and only 12 percent had been terminated from a prior employment for such acts. Again, these findings are consistent with prior *Reports* from 2004 and 2006. (No one should be surprised by the fact that even 1 percent of offenders had a prior criminal record. Pre-employment background investigations, even when done, can be notoriously ineffective at detecting problems with a prospective employee's past. In some instances, this is a result of the inadequacy of the background investigation itself, and in others it is testimony to the skill and ability of employees in "covering their tracks.")

➢   Behavioral signals are an important element in the detection of occupational fraud. The *2009 Report* advises that the two most common indicators were living beyond one's apparent means (39 percent of the incidents) and experiencing financial difficulties at the time of or before the incident (34 percent of the incidents). This might seem "logical" in incidents of fraud, but one might practically ask what it has to do with other forms of risk mismanagement. The answer may be "quite a bit." My colleague, psychiatrist Dr. Daven Morrison, has advised me of a program he has encountered in the course of his work in which the U.S. Navy developed a rating system for personnel scheduled to be deployed aboard ships or submarines. The system rated a number of life events, such as marital problems, personal debt, and recent deaths of family or friends. The premise of the system was that a certain level of personal life stress would impair operational efficiency, no matter how competent the person might be otherwise, and staffing decisions were made accordingly.[3]

A more detailed examination of the ACFE data contained in the *Report* provides further insight into the apparent efficacy of various control mechanisms when dealing with frauds exceeding $1 million and with all fraud cases:

Mechanism by Which Fraud Is Discovered

	$1M+ Incidents	*All Incidents*
Tip	42.3%	46.2%
By Accident	22.8%	20.0%
Internal Audit	18.6%	19.4%
Internal Controls	16.7%	23.3%
External Audit	15.8%	9.1%
Notified by Police	6.0%	3.2%

Sums may add to more than 100 percent because the fraud may have been detected by more than one means at the same time.

Thus, we see that our long-standing and traditional mechanisms such as internal and external audits are less than half as effective in detecting or disclosing frauds as tips. This is not to say they do not have utility; obviously, they do. And we must also remember that some of their function is directed toward objectives other than the detection of fraud (e.g., providing assurance regarding financial statements within the zone of material impact on financial reporting).

When one reclassifies the data to examine frauds committed by owners and executives, a slightly different pattern emerges, but the differences are not dramatic:

	$1M+ Incidents	All Incidents
Tip	51.7%	46.2%
By Accident	17.4%	20.0%
Internal Audit	12.4%	19.4%
Internal Controls	15.2%	23.3%
External Audit	16.3%	9.1%
Notified by Police	3.4%	3.2%

Sums may add to more than 100 percent because the fraud may have been discovered by more than one means at the same time.

Perhaps the most interesting aspect of these data is the sharp drop-off in incidents of $1M fraud detected by internal audit. One can speculate that this is the result of a reluctance to challenge the actions of those in power (internal auditors are, after all, employees) or of the fact that those in power have more ability than lower-level employees to order or manipulate various financial reporting and monitoring mechanisms, thereby making misdeeds more difficult to detect.

These effectiveness rankings seem to be consistent over a variety of business conditions, as shown by analysis of methods of detection in small businesses (those with fewer than 100 employees):

	$1M+ Incidents	All Incidents
Tip	41.7%4	6.2%
By Accident	29.6%	20.0%
Internal Audit	10.7%	19.4%
Internal Controls	17.3%	23.3%
External Audit	14.3%	9.1%
Notified by Police	3.3%	3.2%

Again, percentages may add to more than 100 percent.

Since "tip" seems to consistently be the most common method by which such incidents are detected, ACFE has been kind enough to provide an analysis of the source of these tips, as follows:

Source	Percentage of Incidents
Employee	57.7%
Customer	17.6%
Vendor	12.3%
Shareholder/Owner	9.2%
Anonymous	8.9%
Competitor	1.0%

Sums may add to more than 100 percent.[4]

It thus appears, regardless of organization size, that employees are the richest and most productive source of data regarding fraud issues. I believe it is realistic to assume that this might also hold true for many other forms of risk, such as the misreporting of regulatory data, environmental compliance, working conditions violations, product contamination, and so on. Employees are the most immediate observers of the implementation (or lack thereof) of policies and procedures, tend to be aware of the timeliness with which data are collected and entered into risk management systems, are likely aware of various failings on the part of co-workers, are knowledgeable of short cuts that some may be tempted to take, know who is dissatisfied with corporate policies or managerial actions, and recognize those whose effectiveness and performance may be impacted by personal issues.

While the data set forth here may paint a less-than-flattering picture of traditional risk management mechanisms such as internal audit, internal controls, and external audit as means for detecting fraud, a word of caution is in order. It is very likely these mechanisms detect departures from corporate policies and procedures before they become problems and bring these issues to the attention of management for remedial action. In this regard, they provide a valuable service but probably often do not receive the recognition they deserve. They are in a position like that of police officers who frequently are commended for their bravery and hard work in apprehending wrongdoers but much more rarely are recognized for the amount of crime or risk they prevent.

So, too, with supervisors and managers who, by virtue of their training, experience, and vigilance, detect small issues and deal with them effectively before they become big issues. This is compounded by the human tendency to focus on problems and huge successes, while paying scant attention to those in the middle who keep things on track on a daily basis. These are often the unsung heroes of corporate life. those who help us win a few more games in the middle third, to refer back to sportscaster Mike Francesa's statement.

One issue of note (to be discussed further in Chapters 7 and 8, on organizational intelligence): the *Report* identified customers and vendors as the source of information about an ongoing fraud less than 30 percent of the time, just behind employees. That is pretty powerful and suggests that many corporations may not be casting their risk assessment data-collection net wide enough.

For all its limitations, the AFCE data indicate that there is an element of randomness in the discovery of significant problems. There is a chance that a given employee, on a given day, will decide to report something of interest. Perhaps this decision is the result of a well-crafted compliance program that has educated employees as to the nature of threats to the corporation (recall the interview with Dave Vannort, the former head of SCANA's compliance program, reported in Chapter 3, for his thoughts on how this can be accomplished), enlisted them as "citizen observers" in the effort to monitor and manage such risk, and provided them with convenient and, if need be, anonymous and confidential channels through which to communicate. Providing such programs has certainly been a priority of the security industry since the events of 9/11,[5] but it is unknown how deeply this mindset has penetrated the corporate world since Enron's collapse.

Certainly, auditors, both internal and external, have taken vigorous steps to increase their fraud detection capabilities since the Enron era, supported by the issuance of the Statement of Auditing Standards 99 by the American Institute of Certified Public Accountants in December 2002, but even this measure is geared largely toward the detection of financial misstatement fraud, not all forms of risk. In addition, auditors, by definition, usually come in after the fact and therefore after the harm has been done or at least begun. Employees are much more likely to be on the scene and to see risk forming at its earliest stages.

The bottom line, however, remains. All too often, risk management is a disjointed effort, viewed from various perspectives and in various ways, thus often resulting, as the ACFE data indicate, in discovery by chance. In the next chapter we explore some ideas on how to change this posture.

NOTES

1. Jeffrey Ridley, *Cutting Edge Internal Auditing* (Hoboken, N.J.: Association of Certified Fraud Examiners, 2008).
2. Ibid., pp. 18–24.
3. Duane Jones, "What Really Is Suspicious Activity?" *Security* (April 2008), p. 48.

7.

· ·

ORGANIZATIONAL INTELLIGENCE— PRACTICAL REALITY

· · · · · · · · · · · · · · · ·

Often when I use the term "organizational intelligence," I get one of three reactions—a blank stare, a knowing nod, or a deep sigh.

The blank stare comes from those who simply have not thought about organizations as "intelligent" things; the knowing nod comes from those who think I am referring to "knowledge management" of the collective wisdom of the employees; the deep sigh comes from those who are simply tired of hearing the buzzword of the week from yet another consultant.

Actually, I am referring to none of these things. I am referring to the ability of the organization to understand its risk environment and to harness the abundant resources it already has at its disposal to better assess and respond to it.

Most corporations have a variety of risk assessment tools available to them and, over time, have perhaps become accustomed to them. Therein lies part of the problem. In this chapter I review many of these tools and techniques and provide some thoughts as to why in many instances they do not work or work less well than they should. I discuss some ideas for fixing this and also present some low-cost, low-tech thoughts for new approaches to improve risk assessment capability.

GETTING THE MOST OUT OF HOTLINES

Although they have been around for a while, hotlines took on a new urgency after the Enron meltdown and the advent of the Sarbanes-Oxley legislation. At base, hotlines are simple things—a toll-free telephone number (now increasingly also a computer address) that employees can use to report information of value to the corporation, anonymously if they so choose. This information may be related to financial impropriety, human resources concerns, safety conditions, environmental compliance, employee misconduct, suspected violations of law, conflicts of interest, or deviation from corporate policy and procedures. Some organizations make hotlines available to vendors and customers, also, for they may be valuable sources of useful information. Since each group has a slightly different view of, and relationship to, the corporation, the overall risk assessment environment may benefit from the inclusion of multiple sources.

As useful as hotlines can be, they can also be dangerous if they are poorly implemented or put into use in a simplistic manner. Perhaps the greatest mistake in utilizing a hotline is to "slap it on and turn it loose," without giving thought as to how best to use it. Hotlines are neither a panacea nor a simplistic tool. They are a part, although an important part, of an overall corporate governance, compliance, and risk management system, and they must be monitored to ensure that they are being used to maximum effectiveness. This requires a degree of thought, planning, and coordination, but the results may well be worth the effort many times over.

We have seen from the Association of Certified Fraud Examiners' (ACFE) data presented in Chapter 6 the high percentage of fraud issues that are unearthed by tips. We also have other ACFE data that indicate that having a hotline reduces fraud losses by about 50 percent. It is important to understand this statement. A hotline does not reduce the incidence of fraud—just as many incidents apparently happen. The hotline reduces the duration and therefore the size of the fraud loss. We saw in Chapter 2 the profile of the occupational fraud offender—roughly half are male and half are female; they are well educated, have no criminal records, are middle aged, and have been with the company a number of years—people like most of us. But we also saw that the average fraud ran almost two years before discovery, and the CERT-USSS data discussed in Chapter 2 reveal that usually other people are aware of the fraud. That is the point of the hotline. Through education, monitoring, and careful recruitment, a corporation can reduce the percentage of its employees tempted or inclined by nature to break the rules, but the mere fact of having a good hotline can greatly reduce the damage they do if they do stray.

Perhaps other associations that deal with issues other than fraud, as ACFE does, have data that indicate the effectiveness of hotlines in discovering other forms of risk. Since the field of risk is so broad, it is impossible to poll all possible associations to determine whether ACFE's data reflect an experience that is unique, but an educated hunch says that they reflect a common finding across all kinds of risk. All frauds tend to grow with time, and one suspects that all manner of corporate risk issues follow the same growth curve. Of course it's best to prevent the fraud if you can, but if it occurs, the sooner it is discovered, the better.

Now, more than a few thoughts on hotlines.

Employees' Perceptions of Hotlines

Employees quickly sense how a corporation views and utilizes its hotline. If it is viewed as a necessary evil or given lip service, its value will immediately plunge. Employees talk to each other, and, in the age of the Internet, word can spread quickly, even beyond the confines of the corporation. If legitimate issues reported to the hotline are not addressed in a timely and effective manner, not only will usage decline, but the hotline may be labeled a sham or worse.

Companies fully committed to an effective hotline will take the necessary steps to advertise and promote it. Dave Vannort of SCANA sensed this and acted accordingly, enlisting corporate communications personnel to assist in the process. Other companies have used a variety of tactics, including putting headers on computer screens every time they are activated, printing slogans on pay statements, handing out coffee mugs and note pads with the hotline motto and number on them, and utilizing the normal bulletin board flyers. Training and employee awareness are also important and cannot take a once-a-year, page-in-the-employee-handbook approach. Employees must be educated on the laws, rules, and regulations to which the company is subject, lest they see an issue and not perceive it as such because they lack the necessary knowledge. Obviously, they also need to be aware of company policies and procedures for the same reason.

Avoiding a False Sense of Security

I once had a client that was very proud of its hotline. The chairman of the audit committee had left standing instructions that he was to be called immediately, at any hour of the night or day, if a report of any financial irregularity was received. It all sounded very impressive, so I went to the person responsible for receiving these calls (it was an in-house hotline) and asked how many calls he had received in the previous year. After checking his records he informed me—six calls.

This was a company with 7,000 employees, and in my experience that number of calls was way too low (see the section on human resources later in this chapter). I went to the corporate director of security, with whom I had been working closely on this engagement, and asked him about the hotline. He shook his head and replied that he had called it once himself anonymously to see how well it worked. The first words out of the mouth of the hotline receptionist were "What's your name?"

If other employees had tried to call to report something of concern and got the same question, you can imagine what the reaction would be. It does not take long for word of this to get around a company and for employees to abandon any idea they ever had of making a hotline call. In the meantime, the chairman of the audit committee was sleeping soundly at night because his corporation had a hotline.

The Role of Human Resources

Corporate executives are often surprised when I tell them I believe that the human resources staff is probably the single most important element in selling a hotline to employees. I do this for a reason. Any hotline provider will tell you that well over half of all calls received concern human resources issues such as favoritism, discrimination, conflicts of interest, abusive supervisors, failure to get a raise or promotion, and unpleasant co-workers. These are the normal gamut of personnel issues any organization has to deal with. All too often, these issues are seen by "C suite" executives as a nuisance. In their minds, they put the hotline in to be warned of big, important, financial issues, and now all they get is people complaining about "little" things.

I remind them that these are not "little" issues to the people calling. They are things of great concern to them. Now, the corporation cannot realistically keep everybody happy. Sometimes a call is made by a malcontent or someone out to get a supervisor in trouble for insisting on a full day's work. In other instances, an employee may simply misunderstand corporate policy on a particular human resources issue. But sometimes the complaint is valid, and the facts are sufficient to address it. Common sense tells me that if the corporation takes care of a legitimate complaint that is of concern to an employee, that employee will be more likely to call when she discovers something she believes will be of concern to the corporation.

This is why I sensed there was something wrong in the 7,000-employee corporation that only got six calls in a year. That means that fewer than one in a thousand employees had a human resources issue. Unlikely. Turns out my suspicion was well founded.

Using Outside Providers

Some corporations run internal hotlines, but most contract them out. Internal hotlines have some advantages, since an on-board employee is familiar with corporate culture, operations, staffing, facility locations, and industry issues. There are two downsides though to internal hotlines: they must be staffed 7/24/365, and employees inclined to call may perceive a greater likelihood of losing their cloak of security if they are talking to another employee.

If an outside provider is utilized, there are again pros and cons.

The fees are modest, based upon the size of the corporation, and may run a few dollars a year per employee. Most providers charge on a per-employee basis, and not on the basis of the call volume generated. Around-the-clock, year-round staffing is provided.

Perhaps the single greatest thing to remember about a hotline is that it is only as good as its people. An 800 number is just an 800 number, and an e-mail address is just an e-mail address. The quality of the people receiving the information, especially by telephone, is crucial. A hotline is no better than the people on the receiving end. I have known some hotline providers that try to utilize former or off-duty police officers, as these folks are used to both dealing with people and developing and reporting information in a logical manner. Others use college students and retirees, which is probably not nearly as good unless they go through some fairly detailed training.

Hotline responders can err in any number of ways. They may record information incorrectly or in too vague a manner to be of use in evaluating the situation. They may be too aggressive and scare off the caller. They may be too passive and thereby fail to elicit potentially valuable information.

In evaluating a hotline provider, always ask questions about its staffing: who does it hire, what are the employees' qualifications, what is the turnover rate, what training do employees receive, and so on. These people are your safety net, and that net is only as strong as they are.

Developing the Right Forms

As noted, hotlines are as only as good as the people receiving the communication, but with a little work up front you can improve both their effectiveness and the quality of the information you receive dramatically. It is well worth the minimal investment.

Hotlines receive calls on a wide variety of topics, but some, depending upon your industry, are more important than others. Do not leave hotline responders in the position of having to guess what information and details you would like to know—tell them. Work with your own people and the provider to develop forms that can be kept in a binder or on a computer platform. This way responders will know what types of information they must collect if they receive a call about the X Corporation concerning issue Y. (Even the callers themselves may not be sure of what the company needs to know and may overemphasize one element of their report while ignoring others that may be more important and useful.) Obviously, you will still need a general catch-all form for inquiries and tips that do not fall into any particular category, but you still want to try to capture as much specific information as possible.

If, for example, you want to prepare for a call coming in on a financial issue, work with your financial and accounting people to determine what you would most like to know. The same holds true for human resources, safety, environmental, manufacturing, or any other area you may think is important. The hard work has been done—someone made the call. Make the most of the opportunity.

You may well have an excellent example sitting within your corporation as you read this—bomb threats. For many decades, law enforcement agencies and professional associations have published bomb threat checklists to be used when a call is received. In some corporations, they are widely disseminated to receptionists, administrative assistants, and other personnel likely to receive such calls. If your corporation has a director of security, he is probably aware of these; if not, he can easily access them from various governmental and association websites.

In developing and using such checklists, it is important to follow one rule of thumb—start slow and general, then become more specific. You have the caller on the line, and the caller may be, in fact, the person who planted the bomb, if indeed it even exists. A typical checklist scenario might read as follows (obviously, you would also enter the date and time of the call):

> - Where is the bomb?
> - When is it going to go off?
> - What does it look like?
> - How big is it?
> - Why was it put there?
> - How did you find out about it?
> - Do you know who put it there?

As you can see, if you get accurate answers to only the first two questions, you have enough information to begin notifying the authorities and dealing with the situation. The other questions (and there could be many more) are gravy to help identify those responsi ble and determine who committed the act.

If you follow the same procedure—slow and general moving, then more specific—you will greatly improve the intelligence collection potential of your hotline.

Testing Your Hotline

It is important that you test your hotline at least once a quarter. Hotline providers work shifts since hotlines are twenty-four-hour operations. Call at different times of the day. Are the people working midnight to eight as good as the people on during the day? To compensate for turnover, call regularly—are the people now as good as the ones three months ago?

Prepare fake scenarios and have an employee make an anonymous call to the hotline. You want to check two things: (1) whether the call was reported within the agreed-upon time frame (these can range from immediate, to within an hour, to same day, to next business day), and (2) how accurately the "facts" were written up (some corporations want reporting via facsimile, e-mail, or hard copy, and some want a mixture of two or all of these media). You could miss valuable information if someone on the receiving end failed to record a given fact.

Check also the demeanor of the hotline responder. Was the person too aggressive? Too passive? Indifferent? Rude? All of these things are important, since they will affect the degree to which employees use the hotline and also the value of the information you receive. If you have developed checklists for the provider to use, did the responder follow them?

The hotline is only as good as the people who staff it; make sure you are getting value for your money.

Handling Callbacks

Deciding how to handle callbacks is one of the toughest decisions you will have to make regarding your hotline, and you will probably require consultation with legal counsel, human resources, "C suite" executives, and the board and audit committee. There is no right answer—each corporation must decide what makes sense to them.

From time to time, a caller will ask to be kept informed of what was done with the information she provided. If she chooses to remain anonymous, she can be given a control number to use when calling back so that her subsequent call(s) can be tied to the original call.

You must decide what, if anything, you want to tell callers—or, more accurately, what you want the hotline provider to tell them, since it is doubtful (absent having an in-house hotline) you will get the call. Thus, if you decide to go this route, you may provide the hotline responders with a memo that lays out what you are prepared to tell caller 1797 about situation X on which he called previously. This obviously can be a double-edged sword. Since you have no idea of the identity of the caller, you could be speaking to a newspaper reporter for all you know. On the other hand, if the caller is legitimate, he may have learned additional facts since his initial call, and this could be an excellent time for the responder to gain further information.

There is a variation of this issue that occurs mainly in human resources. You may get a follow-up call that says, "I told you guys about supervisor Z a month ago and he's still here. When are they going to fire him?" Again, how to handle this kind of call is a tough decision, but it is one better made up front than later.

In any event, anonymous callers should be offered a callback identification number, if they so choose. This way, if they develop additional information later, their follow-up call can be easily linked to their initial call.

Designing the Intake Function

Intake, a process common in law enforcement agencies and some corporate functions, is essential in hotline operations. From the perspective of potential liability, the only thing worse than not knowing about an issue or situation is knowing about it and not addressing it. When a hotline call is received and the information seems credible and of sufficient detail, the matter must be assigned to some person or entity for appropriate follow-up. A deadline should be set for resolution of the matter; if need be, the deadline may have to be extended. The point is that hotline matters, once received, cannot become lost in the shuffle or relegated to the "get to it someday" pile, because they can present significant risk. The caller may have taped the call (legally or illegally) or had someone else on the line to listen in. Since the caller can now "prove" that she notified the corporation, her next stop may be a media outlet or an attorney.

Data Retention

All hotline calls should be retained in a database, as should the results of the company's investigation. This may be important for a number of reasons. It allows the corporation to show, in the event of future litigation or regulatory action, that it took the call seriously and responded in what it believed was a timely and appropriate manner. Such a database also allows the corporation to access previous calls in the event of a callback. Perhaps most important, the database allows the corporation to begin to build an intelligence base to better assess its risk environment.

Calls should not only be captured in a database but should be retained in such a manner that they are searchable by a number of different attributes, or fields. These might include date, time, type of issue reported, names mentioned, units or facilities mentioned, persons believed to have knowledge of the activity, time frame in which the alleged activity took place, and the name of the supervisor of the unit in question. This will permit a future search using bits and pieces of information gathered in future calls to see if patterns emerge. Such a capability will markedly improve the corporation's ability to develop more informed assessments of possible risk issues.

Incident Analysis

Following on the discussion about retention, corporations would be wise to think even more broadly about risk. Risk tends to be in corporate silos—the general counsel handles some, the audit committee handles some, the internal audit function handles some, human resources handles some, corporate security handles some, safety and environmental personnel handle some, and so on. It is the rare corporation that pulls all this information together in one place where it can be analyzed for trends and patterns. It is possible a given supervisor or a given unit has had four different issues within the past year, but, since they were handled by different corporate functions, they never get connected. The same can be said for functions. Perhaps sales or distribution has problems across a number of units or divisions, but these never get grouped and analyzed. The issue is very similar to the ABC (apple, bushel, crop) phenomenon discussed earlier and is tied to the phenomenon of "looking sideways." Without adequate data, analysis is seriously weakened.

Staffing

Installing a hotline or making an existing hotline more effective can impose a sudden and significant drain on the corporate entities tasked with following up on complaints or reports. Corporate staffs are typically busy as is, so the sudden appearance of two or three new issues to be dealt with in a timely manner can be disruptive. Corporations need to plan for this. There are a number of ways to address it: less-sensitive projects can be put on hold; people can work overtime; resources can be temporarily diverted from other entities to augment the department in question; former departmental employees can be retained as temporary or part-time staff; or outside assistance can be sought. The options vary, but the message is consistent—something must be done with the complaint or issue. The worst-case scenario is that the issue gets ignored, sits for a prolonged period of time, during which it may mushroom, or is handled in such a perfunctory manner that investigators never get to its core.

Public Reporting

Some organizations, including the FBI, have adopted a policy of publicizing the results of internal investigations of alleged misconduct, albeit without the names of those involved. They do this for several reasons. It makes clear to the employee population that such matters are taken seriously and will be followed up on. It sends a clear message to all employees as to what sorts of conduct are impermissible and the consequences thereof. It promotes more active reporting. And, it serves as an alert to supervisors and managers as to what may be brewing within their realms of responsibility.

There are downsides to this policy, such as the possibility that the investigation and the actions based upon it will leak beyond the corporate walls, even, perhaps, to the press. Adopting such a policy is a decision that must be weighed carefully, but there are advantages to it, especially in an age that values "transparency."

OTHER RISK MANAGEMENT TOOLS

While hotlines are valuable, they are but one tool in a suite of corporate governance, compliance, and risk management processes. They need to be integrated with all the other facets of the system. We now turn to some risk management processes that are sometimes not used as effectively as they might be. We also explore some options that are a bit unusual.

Internal Audits

As noted earlier, in most corporations internal audit faces a number of infrastructure issues that limit its effectiveness. Among these are workload, travel, perception within the corporation, staff experience and training, promotional opportunities, use as a rotational assignment, and the need to execute an ambitious audit plan each year under tight deadlines. If internal audit is viewed as the primary function of the corporation for spotting issues of risk, it may not be up to the task. One can hope that it is, but in fact it is one of several risk-sensing and management mechanisms. Consideration should be given to the role that internal audit is expected to play and a realistic analysis made of whether it has the staffing, training, and experience to perform that role.

External Audits

The use of an external audit may be something of a mixed bag. It may be required because of a number of factors: company policy, regulatory policies, or a desire for improved corporate governance. In any event, it can be time-consuming and expensive.

External audit staff can bring substantial value, although at a cost. Companies can use productive strategies to gain more bang for the buck from them. Typically, an audit engagement is staffed with one audit partner, one senior manager, two or more managers, and a number of audit staff. In very large corporations, these numbers may increase substantially. These outside auditors at the corporation's location may be at the site full or part time; time spent on site generally varies by rank, with an audit partner, except in very large corporations, present only part time, because they have other audit clients to service. Audit partners receive oral and e-mail updates from the on-scene audit staff and make periodic in-person visits. As the partner in charge of the audit, they are the main point of contact with the audit client.

The staff may be at the corporate site much more frequently and it is not unusual for them to work on-site full time for prolonged periods. The key to the system is the managers, especially the senior manager. The managers have the most contact with the "troops," the audit staff, and have the deepest knowledge of their work and what has developed from it. They are, however, relatively young and typically have about five to seven years' experience. They, in turn, brief the senior manager frequently. The senior manager is a different story. Typically someone with ten or more years' experience, senior managers have been involved in more than 100 audits and are in many cases partners-to-be.

Frequent, casual "How's it going?" visits with the on-site senior manager may be a rich source of information, as audit personnel frequently encounter issues and information beyond the scope of the audit itself that may never make into the final audit report. They can serve as a fresh set of eyes looking at the corporation and help identify potential risk issues.

Corporate Security

In days past, corporate security was normally a field of locks, alarms, and guards. That has changed dramatically in the past twenty or so years, and corporate security staff are now often involved in activities as varied as protection of intellectual property, detection of brand counterfeiting and diversion, risk assessment, crisis management planning and training, disaster recovery, executive protection, foreign threat assessment, facilities design, and more. Given their broad mandate, which continues to expand, they tend to become involved in almost every aspect of the corporation. In addition, since many security officers have backgrounds in law enforcement or intelligence and also belong to professional associations, they can tap into a wide range of expertise in other corporations. One organization in particular, the International Security Managers Association (ISMA), is composed of the top corporate security executives in the world, with a membership of no more than 300 or 400. Yet, for so limited a membership, it is an incredibly rich source of information. I was a member for a number of years and participated in its secure website discussions. On many occasions, I saw posts from members along the lines of "We're building a new facility in Argentina. Can anyone recommend a reliable perimeter security, alarm, and guard company?" Usually there were three or four responses within an hour or two.

ISMA is a valuable association and serves as a portal to a vast store of knowledge and experience. The director of security of any corporation of any size should belong to it.

Overseas Security Advisory Council

The Overseas Security Advisory Council (OSAC), run by the U.S. Department of State, has been in existence for well over twenty years. Its website is free and available to the public and provides a daily update of risk factors—terrorism, political instability, recent incidents, economic conditions, travel conditions, and more. It is an excellent source of risk information pertaining to foreign countries. The annual meeting of OSAC in Washington, D.C., is attended by a veritable who's who of the corporate security world.

Anonymous Calls and Letters

For all the work I have done with corporations, large, medium, and small, I have yet to see one that had a formal, articulated policy about how anonymous communications should be handled. They can come in all forms—letters, telephone calls, e-mails, voicemails—and they can go to anyone. We sometimes assume that someone who has a complaint or issue will call the right person or department, but that well may not happen. An unhappy client may call anyone—perhaps customer service—to complain about a totally unrelated issue. Without a coherent policy in place that sets out how such communications are to be handled and that has been provided to all employees, each employee is left to make his own best-guess judgment as to what to do.

News Articles

Often we assume that any news item of importance will be known to us if we read one of the major metropolitan papers or scan the major databases. This may well not be the case, as potentially important developments may be reported in small, regional outlets or on more obscure websites. The technology exists to harvest this information and there are companies that for a fee will scan the entire Internet using a form of keywords for news or even e-mails pertaining to your corporation. Thus, if you are the X corporation, you may wish to search for any reference to it that links to the words "fraud," "misstatement," "cooking the books," "bomb," or any other words or phrases.

Sales Force

We usually think of the sales force as a distribution channel, putting information on the street and producing sales as a result, but it can also be a powerful information-gathering tool. Sales personnel deal with customers, dealers, and distributors every day and hear what is going on in the marketplace, what competitors are up to, who is doing well and who is not. Some companies have used the feedback from their sales forces very well, enabling them to compete more successfully in the marketplace and to avoid surprises.

Public Relations

We tend to think of the public relations department, like the sales force, as a distribution channel, but it can also provide useful information. From the tone and frequency of inquiries the staff get, they may sense that something is developing out there, perhaps something the corporation would benefit from knowing about sooner rather than later. Sensitizing public relations staff to risk issues the corporation is concerned with may pay off in early warning of an impending issue.

Vendors

A fair number of corporations make hotlines available to vendors, as well as to employees and customers. Vendors can be an excellent source of information, as they almost always deal with other clients, some of whom may be competitors. While one would not ask a vendor to betray another client's confidentiality, vendors may still be able to provide some idea of what they are hearing and seeing in the marketplace. They may also, in the worst-case scenario, have information about misconduct on behalf of corporate employees, from asking for or hinting about kickbacks to sloppy performance in setting up orders and specifications.

Asking "Dumb" Questions

In both the marketplace and within our corporate environments there is a reluctance to ask a "dumb" question, one to which the answer appears so "obvious" that asking it reflects poorly upon our apparently substandard intelligence. This, press reports advise, was the root of much of the success of the Madoff operation. Since so many apparently smart, sophisticated, and financially savvy people had invested with Madoff, one would appear obtuse if she asked the basic question "How exactly do you generate profits?"

In a *USA Today* article, Seth Freeman discusses this phenomenon and recounts an interesting story. Bethany McLean, a reporter for *Fortune* magazine, once interviewed a high-flying and prominent CFO and asked him how his company made money. Incensed, the CFO attacked her and called her an ill-prepared incompetent to even ask so basic a question. Undeterred, she went forward with the article she was working on.

The CFO was Jeff Skilling, the company was Enron, and McLean's was the first article to question the business practices of that company.[1]

Think about the several examples of corporations that gave out "good news" that later turned out to be false. Our failure to question good news that somehow seems too good to be true can perhaps be attributed to our fear of looking "dumb." Thus, risk goes unnoticed and unchecked.

Exit Interviews

We return to human resources once again, although a fair number of exit interviews are conducted by operational supervisors rather than by human resources staff. Generally, the exit interview is viewed as sort of a pro forma thing: the signing of some forms and the collection of company property. Once in a while, there may a perfunctory question about the state of corporate operations, but it is usually asked without much emphasis or enthusiasm.

A couple of well-crafted exit interview questions can pay big dividends, as some employees will disclose information for the good of the corporation and others will do so out of a sense of spite, anger, or revenge. For workers who are leaving, it is safe to speak more freely, since they are out the door and have new employment. It is doubtful many people will say much of value, but, if only one in a hundred does, it is still a good rate of return for a minimal investment.

We never know why someone will decide to say or do something, no matter how well we may think we know the person. The purpose of risk-oriented questions in an exit interview is not to grill employees on their way out the door. Rather, it is to open the door with a few focused but nonthreatening questions and to see if the person chooses to walk through it.

There is sometimes a tendency to dismiss human forms of intelligence gathering in favor of quantitative data that we can capture electronically, then slice and dice to our heart's content. People are more complex than that, and I have often posed a question in classes and presentations to those convinced that if it cannot be quantified, it does not count. I ask these students to go home and pull out the quantitative data files they used to make two of the most important decisions in their lives: who they married, and how many children they had. Surely, such important and life-changing events were the subject of substantial analysis—but I doubt it.

We overlook the human side of intelligence gathering, as the 9/11 Commission found, at our own risk. Perhaps I am more attuned to such issues because of the many years I spent as an FBI agent and forensic consultant. We live on interviews and what people can tell us. We become expert at deducing how much personal knowledge an interview can provide and also their motivations for sharing or not sharing that information with us. It is the nature of our trade, and, while we certainly use automated systems for various tasks, they cannot always tell us what we need to know. The only difference between manslaughter (as when someone is struck by a vehicle) and murder is intent. You have a dead body either way.

Sometimes intent can be inferred through data analysis, but it's much better and much easier if you can get someone to admit it.

As I noted, many corporate security personnel are former law enforcement officers who have fine interrogation skills. But, in the hundreds of corporate investigations I have been involved in, only once did I encounter a corporate security personnel who was part of the internal team. Usually, the corporate team is made up of attorneys and people from internal audit. Why corporations do not use this in-house security resource more often is beyond me.

Here is a case in point. I was retained by an investment group that had just bought a chain of retail outlets and, at the last minute, had heard a rumor that the books had been cooked. The investors swallowed hard, completed the deal, and called us in to try to get to the bottom of the rumor. I convinced them to do something unusual. Certainly, we had teams of forensic accountants scouring the books, but I wanted to try a new tack. I met with the new ownership, the new general counsel, and the existing director of human resources. I suggested we jointly pick ten former employees on the basis of the positions they had held with the company, the length of their time with the company, and the reasons they had left. In the space of an hour, we had our selections made.

In the space of a week, I had located six of the ten who were still in the general vicinity, and four of them agreed to meet with me. Of the four, two told me how the books had, in fact, been cooked. I was then able to go back to the forensic accountants and tell them where to look to verify the assertions, thus saving hundreds of hours that would have been spent looking at everything to find the problem. As it turned out, the investigators were able to verify the allegations and so advise the client, who initiated remedial action against the former owners.

I do not recommend this technique to the inexperienced. The

wrong approach or technique in such a situation can make the problem substantially worse. You do not want to start rumors in the local community where the company is based or in the greater financial community, where it must operate on a daily basis. I "solved" this problem by simply stating that my firm had been retained by the new ownership to take a look at the financial controls in place to see if they needed to be updated or modified. All I did was open the door. Two people decided to step through it. So, too, with exit interviews—a door opened may get some traffic.

In the course of many engagements for clients, I have consistently been amazed at how often they had signs of an impending problem but failed to see it before it became full blown. These are not dumb people, but they missed what later was so obvious. One is left to wonder why. In some cases there was a primary reason, but it more often appeared that there was a combination of factors, as Bill Parrett, formerly of Deloitte & Touche LLP, has so wisely noted. Sometimes, big things hurt you, but more often the cause is an unfortunate combination of two or more smaller things, much like the aircraft accidents I once reviewed.

In this book I have described some of the most common contributing factors I have seen:

> Misunderstood or outdated business models (growth by acquisition case study)
> Too-rapid consolidation and downsizing of control mechanisms (retail chain study)
> Background noise (property casualty company study)
> Trusting unrealistic good news (credit card company and wholesale company case studies)
> False sense of security (property casualty company study)
> Not living the code of "tone at the top" ("Dave" case study)

> ➤ Failure to utilize and organize available organizational intelligence

To me this means that we should perhaps be a bit more like the squirrel, scanning 360 degrees at least some of the time and using a more complete suite of scanning tools, many of which we already have.

"Covert" Operations

I don't want to sound like I am advocating a James Bond mentality, but covert operations can be both immensely practical and useful. Many years ago, I had a friend who was a high-flying computer guy who was courted by any number of companies that wanted him to leave his current job and join with them. One job in particular appealed to him, and, although it was in Canada, on the surface it appeared to be a once-in-a-lifetime opportunity. He would get a huge bump in pay, his relocation expenses would be covered, and he would be given equity in this young company that believed it was poised to be the "next big thing" in computer technology. Over a number of weeks, he made trips to Canada to meet with the owners, the CEO, and principal officers and also to learn exactly what his role and responsibility would be. The time had come for his last trip before the company would decide whether to make him an offer, but he fudged a little bit. His final interview would be over by 4 P.M., and there was an available flight home at 6:30 P.M.

To that point, everything had seemed beautiful—these people were bright and energetic; they had promising technology, a sound business plan, and adequate financing and were ready to take on the world, but he wanted to check one more time. He purposely booked a flight that did not leave until 9 P.M. and, following his interview, hung out in a spare office, ostensibly to make phone calls and catch up on paperwork. At 6 P.M. he emerged from the office and walked through the company's space. No one was there. This was not what he expected from a company ready to take on the world.

The next day he politely declined the job offer. A year later, the company was out of business.

Another friend used a bit more aggressive technique when evaluating the profitability of a bar and restaurant he was thinking of buying. He parked near the location very early in the morning, and, as trucks stopped to make deliveries, he bribed the drivers to tell him how much they delivered and how often. A twenty-dollar bill usually did the trick. He eventually bought the establishment but was able to negotiate a much more favorable price than the financials would have suggested, on the basis of the information he had.

Lest one think such behavior is limited only to several of my strange friends, *The Wall Street Journal* reports that such covert behavior is becoming increasingly common among executives debating corporate moves. The article notes a survey by BlueSteps, an arm of the Association of Executive Search Consultants, that reports that, since 2005, nearly half of the 1,145 U.S. executives polled had secretly visited locations of a potential employer to assess their mode of operation and the quality of their people. The survey noted that this is common in the retail industry but is spreading to banking, restaurants, and manufacturing.[2]

NOTES

1. Seth Freeman, "Ask the 'Dumb' Questions," *USA Today*, January 13, 2009, p. 11A.
2. Joann S. Lublin, "Job Seekers Go Undercover to Check Out Employers," *Wall Street Journal*, November 24, 2008, p. B-4.

8.

· ·

ORGANIZATIONAL INTELLIGENCE— THOUGHT AND THEORY

· · · · · · · · · · · · · · · · · ·

This chapter discusses some theories about organizational intelligence and also some techniques that seem to work to harness and organize it. There are literally scores of such theories and techniques, and this is by no means an attempt to analyze them all. These are merely the ones that, in my experience, seem to be practical and bring clarity to the process.

COMPSTAT: THE NYPD'S NEW RADAR

If you have responsibility for managing risk, you probably think you have a difficult job, and I am sure you do, but try policing New York City. With more than 8 million residents and a similar number of people commuting into the city every day to work, shop, or sightsee, it is a formidable task. Then throw in the United Nations, with all its peculiar demands and issues; the fact that New York City is still an active port; the city's status as the financial and media capital of the world; a subway system that stretches hundreds of miles and carries millions of passengers a day; a resident and visiting population that represents every cultural, political, racial, religious, and linguistic variation in the world; Manhattan's status as an island, accessible only by bridge or tunnel; chaotic traffic conditions; one of the world's largest diamond districts and any number of high-end retail stores, all with lots of nice stuff to shoplift, burgle, or steal; five La Cosa Nostra "families" and any number of ethnically based gangs; an aging infrastructure prone to water main breaks, steam explosions that send manhole covers dozens of feet into the air, and bridge components that collapse; constant construction or repair projects being conducted in already tight spaces; and any city's fair share of crooks, hookers, panhandlers, drunks, dopers, crazies, and despondent suicidal cases with lots of bridges and tall buildings to ponder. It is a task.

Over the years, the New York Police Department (NYPD) has done an excellent job of staying on top of all this activity, but in the mid-1980s it took a giant step forward that proved so successful that it has been widely duplicated in any number of police departments around the country—it introduced COMPSTAT, an acronym for computer comparison statistics.

In his book *The Compstat Paradigm*, Vincent E. Henry, a twenty-year veteran of the NYPD who had been intimately associated with the COMPSTAT program, recounts his observations about it. He notes, with pride, that the program won the 1996 Innovations in American Government Award, bestowed by the Ford Foundation and the John F. Kennedy School of Government at Harvard University.[1] At base, the program is both an analytical tool for gauging management effectiveness at the precinct level and a technique for assigning resources where they are most needed. In this regard, Henry compares it to the performance of the Royal Air Force against German bombers in World War II. Assisted by newly perfected radar warnings, a relatively small number of British pilots were able to inflict serious damage on the attacking German forces.[2] Likewise, the NYPD was able to use its "radar" (improved and coordinated statistical analysis) to assign police officers, detectives, and specialized units where the need and the number of targets (criminals) were greatest. At least in part because of COMPSTAT, crime fell so much that New York City was safer on a per capita statistical basis than Orlando, Atlanta, Salt Lake City, Denver, and St. Louis.[3]

Much of this success was a result of the efforts of a highly innovative man, Jack Maples, who was appointed Deputy Commissioner of Crime Control Strategies by then–Police Commissioner William Bratton. Maples, a brilliant if eccentric student of military history, understood the value of timely intelligence in military victory and applied some military concepts to the field of law enforcement. The program that evolved was a descendent of the pin maps long used by police agencies to plot crime, as often seen in old police movies. Maples and his team brought this system into the twentieth century by moving it to a paradigm that provided both the ecology and the spatial distribution of crime. Further, in addition to deploying resources, in disguise if need be, detectives started debriefing arrestees, inquiring about their associates and their areas of activity. This seemingly simple step was actually a large one, since previously a crime was "cleared" with the arrest of a single perpetrator. No effort was made to gain valuable associational and tracking intelligence about other probable perpetrators.[4] The reader might note that this is similar to the practice I described as "looking sideways." Just as the police make a single arrest, in corporations we are all familiar with dealing with the "bad apple" and then "moving on." Failure to look sideways ensures that the next bad apple will surface sooner rather than later.

One should not assume that the NYPD's implementation of COMPSTAT was the result of some massive outlay for outside professional assistance; it was not. It was done with off-the-shelf software packages and either a few PCs or a basic LAN system, largely developed in-house.

But COMPSTAT quickly evolved into much more than a tracking and deployment tool; it became a management philosophy and system in and of itself. One of the people "there at the beginning" was John Gilmartin, who has been kind enough to share his thoughts.

MANAGEMENT BY COMPSTAT

The COMPSTAT concept used by the NYPD was widely hailed throughout the law enforcement community as a key element in obtaining a dramatic reduction in crime rate in a huge, unruly city often noted for its high rate of crime. COMPSTAT was first implemented in the mid-1990s by the Management Information Systems (MIS) division of the NYPD, which was headed at that time by John Gilmartin. Gilmartin, who would spend thirty-seven years with the NYPD and who would eventually retire as assistant chief, is largely credited with building up COMPSTAT. He has provided much of the information in this section.

The emergence of COMPSTAT at this time must be put into perspective. In the 1980s, police departments around the country were beginning to move toward the fairly new concept of "community policing" (getting closer to the citizens and getting all organizations involved in addressing what had been previously considered purely "police" problems) and toward acceptance of "broken-windows theory." This theory was first enunciated in a March 1982 article in *Atlantic Monthly* magazine that was written by James Q. Wilson, a distinguished criminologist at Harvard who at a young age already held a chair, and George Kelling, a noted law enforcement writer, scholar, and researcher. The article, entitled "The Police and Neighborhood Safety: Broken Windows," changed the face of U.S. law enforcement forever. Its premise was simple but profound. It argued that if a broken window in a building was not repaired, it would lead to more broken windows. Eventually, the entire tone of the neighborhood would decline, because no one seemed to care about maintaining structures or standards. This, in turn, would create an environment for more serious crimes to take place.

Over time, the concept has evolved into what is now known as "quality-of-life" policing. The police are on the street every day and see many things, some of which at first glance do not appear to be "police" problems. The police can fix some of these. For others, they must enlist the assistance of the neighborhood or other city agencies. This doesn't seem to be the stuff of police work, but it is remarkably effective in reducing serious crimes. An example may be instructive.

The five boroughs of New York City are linked by many forms of transportation, but none perhaps as important as the subway system. Spanning hundreds of miles of track and carrying millions of passengers a day, the subway system is the veins and arteries of a huge city. However, for many years, the system was also a dangerous place. Muggings and purse snatchings were common, and a murder every now and then was hardly unheard of.

The police, as one might suspect, responded. They put more uniformed officers on the platforms and in the subway cars. They did "saturation policing" in particularly bad areas, concentrating a large number of officers in small areas. They tried using undercover officers, who posed as drunks, sleeping commuters, or quiet house-wives. Certainly, they made their fair share of arrests, but the crime rates did not move much. Then, following the concepts of broken-windows theory, they tried something new.

From time immemorial, "fare beating" has been common in the New York City subway system. Back in the days when a waist-high turnstile was the only thing between a potential passenger and the train, some passengers, mainly young males, would hop over the turnstile rather than put a token into it to gain admittance. The cops starting watching the turnstiles and arresting those who chose to hop them. Crime went down. The cops made more arrests. Crime went down even more. By this simple device (take care of the little things and you will take care of the bigger things), the police af-fected subway crime rates dramatically.

It was during this era that John Gilmartin ran the MIS division of the NYPD. We have seen all the old police and detective movies, where on the wall is a map with small colored pins in it to indicate the locations where various crimes have been committed. By the early 1990s, the pins had been replaced by informal systems. Often computer-based but usually run on a precinct-by-precinct basis, these systems were used to track crime in various neighborhoods. The problem was that the system was not coordinated: some precincts used it and others did not; the formats they used varied; the data collected were never pulled together to form a "map" of the entire city. Then COMPSTAT (for "computer statistics") was born. COMPSTAT was configured to map crime in various forms in every precinct in the city, from "quality of life" issues like aggressive pan-handling and running of stop signs up to the most serious offenses, such as rape and murder. In addition to community policing and broken-windows theory, the city needed COMPSTAT to get crime under control. New York City was coming off some rough times in the 1970s. The number of murders could top 2,000 a year, and in a bad precinct it was not unusual to have two or three homicides in a single night.

Once COMPSTAT got established, it provided a much more uniform and detailed map of the city and its crime issues. As time went on, other statistics were included, such as officers' use of sick days. (A higher-than-average number of sick days taken in a precinct could be an indication of morale problems.)

While COMPSTAT was certainly a data management system (largely self-built, by the way), it was much more than that. The weekly or biweekly COMPSTAT meetings were seen by precinct commanders as either an opportunity or a nightmare. The meetings often lasted two or three hours, and only a handful of precinct commanders were summoned to appear at any given meeting, usually on fairly short notice. The large room would be filled with all the brass: the chief of patrol, the chief of detectives, the "super chiefs" who commanded various parts of the NYPD infrastructure, and bosses from specialty units, such as narcotics, public morals, and the like. There were fifty or sixty people in the room when the precinct commanders were asked to explain their numbers and what they were doing about them. Lack of knowledge and weak answers were not tolerated, and many a precinct commander spent some very unhappy times being picked apart by the higher-ups. Some of the questions were fairly simple: if you have a severe burglary problem in your precinct from 2 A.M. to 6 A.M., why is your anticrime team working the four-to-twelve shift?

At the same time, the NYPD would use these numbers and these meetings to make resource allocation decisions. The Public Morals division might be detailed to a given precinct to address a prostitution or an after-hours drinking problem. Similarly, narcotics or auto theft resources might be deployed. Some high-intensity force might be brought to bear through a program called "Pressure Point," which infused large numbers of eager young recruits fresh from the Police Academy into a given precinct.

Such was the history and utility of COMPSTAT, and its lessons may hold value for the modern corporation, which, when faced with dynamic and far-flung operations, often has no central data source help it determine where problems are beginning to build.

There may be a tendency to see the law enforcement/COMPSTAT model as being inappropriate or inadequate for a multinational corporation, since, after all, even a city as large as New York is only a city, which occupies one geographic area and is not dispersed around the globe. But cities are hugely complex; each is composed of scores of neighborhoods with different economic, ethnic, religious, social, and cultural characteristics. Then, too, crime respects no boundaries. A criminal does not focus on the fact that he may commit his crime in Queens, New York, or, perhaps no more than a block or two away, in neighboring Nassau County, which does not fall within the city's boundaries. There is no bright painted line that divides the two. For this reason, many police departments now routinely share information and intelligence with neighboring jurisdictions, much like a corporation's manufacturing facility in India might share information with the corporate headquarters in Chicago.[5]

WHAT WE CAN LEARN FROM LAW ENFORCEMENT

As I stated earlier with reference to the COMPSTAT program, I believe that corporations can learn much from the experience of law enforcement agencies. They have been handling risk (ours) for centuries and have gotten progressively better at finding what works. There are any number of innovative programs in place throughout the country, and one of them is in my own backyard, Brunswick County, North Carolina.

The Brunswick County Sheriff's Office (BCSO) is an old institution that has grown greatly as the county (one of the twenty fastest-growing in the United States) itself has expanded. Under the leadership of John W. Ingram V, a new, innovative sheriff, the BCSO is launching new programs at a rapid clip. One, called "Citizen Observers," has a component called "Alert Network" that does two interesting things: it seeks the assistance of citizens in solving cases, and it alerts them to possible risks so that they can better protect themselves. It does this through four interrelated programs:

1. **Citizen Alerts.** These inform citizens of public safety issues; provide information about crime trends; furnish descriptions of fugitives and missing persons; and give advice on personal safety and protection of property.

2. **Business Alerts.** These alerts provide information about crimes that are pertinent to particular types of businesses.

3. **Case Alerts.** Case alerts allow the BCSO to disseminate information about ongoing investigations to those persons who have voluntarily registered to be citizen observers.

4. **Watch Group Alerts.** These provide information to specific neighborhoods about criminal activity in their immediate area.

To quote from a flyer on the program, "Possibly the biggest benefit of the Alert Network is the way it makes possible two-way communication between law enforcement and the public."

This, in my experience, is a process uncommon in many corporations: the harnessing of the employees as "citizens" of the corporation to assist in the management of risk, and the provision of information to them about pertinent risk issues.

We perhaps can learn a lot from law enforcement.

CONNECTING IT TO BUSINESS NEEDS

For all the promise of information systems and technology, some observers blame the "computer" folks for many of our problems. The renowned management theorist Peter Drucker lay many problems squarely on their doorstep: "A new Information Revolution is well under way. It has started in business enterprise, and with business information. . . . And what has triggered these information revolutions and is driving them is the failure of the 'Information Industry'—the IT people, the MIS people, the CIO's—to provide INFORMATION."[6]

I respectfully disagree, at least in part, with Mr. Drucker. Certainly, I, like many others, have seen IT folks make their share of missteps—doing something because they can; tending to always chase the "next new thing"; "excluding" data because they "did not fit"; failing to fully understand and appreciate the ultimate objective; and coming to love the technology more. On the other hand, I have seen more problems created at the top and the bottom of corporations. At the top, the "C suite," I have often noted a failure to fully appreciate or fund risk and a false sense of security. At the bottom, I have seen too much junk and background noise in data that, no matter how well presented, still seem to reflect junk or background noise.

At the same time, we must allow for the penchant of IT people, like most others, to live in their world and to see the rest of the world through their window on it. Ross, Weill, and Robertson, in their book *Enterprise Architecture as Strategy*, note the following after spending five years studying information architecture transformations: "ineffectiveness of IT architecture efforts . . . has troubled us for years . . . we have railed against traditional IT architecture efforts for their remoteness from the reality of business and their heavy reliance on mind-numbing detail in charts that look more like circuit diagrams than business descriptions."[7] They then go on to prescribe a process for building a "foundation for execution" in support of business objectives:

> ➤ Analyze your existing foundation for execution.
> ➤ Define your operating model.
> ➤ Design your enterprise architecture.
> ➤ Set priorities.
> ➤ Design and implement an engagement model.
> ➤ Exploit your foundation for growth.[8]

One may choose to follow this tack or another, but the point is that you need a well-thought-out process based upon substantial analysis and executed in accordance with a master plan. Technology for the sake of technology will not suffice; nor will knee-jerk or ad hoc "solutions."

THE POWER OF DATA MINING

Some corporations go to extraordinary lengths to mine their existing data, and other corporations even make a business of mining public-source and proprietary data and selling the resulting analysis to yet other corporations. In his book *The Numerati*, Stephen Baker recounts the evolution and utility of this approach:

➤   Baker recounts the exploits of Dave Morgan, the founder of Tacoda, which tracks Web surfing. His company follows the Web-surfing activities of 150 million people and usually sells their results to advertising executives, including the unusual (but commonsensical) patterns they have found. More than 20 billion behavioral clues are analyzed—a day! For example, the company has found a relationship between those searching obituaries and those renting cars. Upon reflection, the logic is there, but it is not apparent to the casual viewer—that those who discover that a distant friend or relative has died may decide to attend the funeral or memorial services and, upon arriving at their destination, may well need to rent a car.

➤   Interestingly, the same search/linking techniques also show a relationship between those who visit websites for romantic books and movies and those who rent cars. Evidently, those interested in romance are more inclined to rent vehicles for romantic "getaway" weekends than those who do not.

➤   Baker refers to the notorious but highly effective East German intelligence service, Stasi, which employed tens of thousands of informants to keep track of their associates, friends, and even relatives and to report activities unacceptable to the state. He notes that today, we, as consumers and Internet users, actually spy on ourselves by leaving an audit and behavioral trail that others skilled in tracking such things can follow.

➤   In a given month, Yahoo mines 110 billion bits of information about its users—what they do, when they do it, how often they do it. Each person visiting Yahoo's network of advertisers leaves, on average, 2,520 clues as to her interests. While this represents a massive amount of potentially useful data, much of it is noise. Directed searches of these data are the key, reducing the search time required by a factor of 30,000, from twenty-four hours to three seconds.

➤ Carnegie-Mellon University published a study that indicated if you have the gender, date of birth, and zip code of a person, you could obtain the name of 87 percent of the U.S. population.

➤ Computers have permitted companies to increasingly monitor workers' performance activity, especially when they are on their computers. Microsoft, in 2006, filed for a patent to protect a technology for assessing the physical responses of employees to stress, revealed through such manifestations as blood pressure and psychological state.

The list could go on, but I hope that these tidbits offer some idea of the power and uses of data mining.[9]

Other companies have picked up on this technique. In his article "Mining for Gold," Ben Worthen recounts the work of Sean Kelley and others at Deutsch Bank as they make use of the data-rich environment surrounding us all. Kelley, in an interview, observes that there are more than 100 million blogs out there, and this number doubles every six and one-half months. Ninety-five percent of their content is "noise," useless for collecting organizational intelligence and crafting corporate strategy. Creating the right algorithms to find the "emotions of the market" is key to gaining what others refer to as "actionable intelligence."[10]

THE EIGHT CRITICAL ENVIRONMENTS OF KARL ALBRECHT

The writer, theorist, consultant and speaker Karl Albrecht has produced some intriguing thoughts and concepts as to how organizations can better understand their environments. One of his concepts is "The Eight Critical Environments" of a corporation or other organization (think of them as pieces of a circle surrounding the organization):

1. **Customer Environment**—Who they are, what they are thinking, what they need, how they behave, what they value.
2. **Competitor Environment**—Who they are, what their strengths and weaknesses are, how they tend to behave.
3. **Economic Environment**—What is going on in markets and economies, and what is happening with capital, costs, resources, currency, and the like.
4. **Technological Environment**—What trends and developments are taking place.
5. **Social Environment**—What elements are present in cultures and societies and where they develop and manifest themselves.
6. **Political Environment**—From local to regional to state to national governments, what their priorities and policies are, what imperatives they respond to, and how these play into their public-policy decisions.
7. **Legal Environment**—From labor issues to intellectual property to environmental concerns and beyond, how trends in laws and litigation affect the business enterprise.
8. **Physical Environment**—The likely impact of all physical factors, from weather to natural resources to transportation infrastructure to availability of skilled labor.[11]

In his book, Albrecht goes on to discuss the issue of opportunities and threats and notes, correctly, I believe, that many times they can be one and the same, depending upon how they are perceived and acted upon.[12] I appreciate his recognition of these factors but believe I would include risk as part of the corporate environment, thereby adding a ninth element. Certainly, in his conceptualization, risk is inherent in all of the eight elements he identifies, but, perhaps because of a personal prejudice based on many years of dealing with risk, I would recognize it separately. It is not easy to capture the risk that comes from a false sense of security, from data skewed because of performance metrics, the treachery that resides in the hearts of some, the danger of too-rapid growth or consolidation, and false baselines. Within his framework, a separate category for risk as yet another significant environmental factor might provide a more holistic view. Where, for example, do we capture the risk from the fact that someone may fail to properly clean a machine in a peanut-processing plant?

In a subsequent book, *Corporate Radar*, Albrecht further refines his theories and also provides some cautions that directly parallel my own thinking and experiences. He discusses, for example, the need to question assumptions, challenge data, double-check and confirm information sources, and develop specific lines of inquiry capable of being answered. Indeed, Albrecht does an excellent job in going beyond the issues I recount from experience; he discusses statistical misperceptions common in everything from financial reporting to international trade.[13]

Albrecht has produced numerous other works on the subject of organizational intelligence, among them two papers available on his website (Karl.Albrecht.com): "The Triune Intelligence Model" and "Organizational Intelligence and Knowledge Management: Thinking Outside the Silos." I recommend them to those interested in further exploring the fascinating but sometimes complex world of organizational intelligence.[14]

NOTES

1. Vincent E. Henry, *The Compstat Paradigm* (Flushing, N.Y.: Looseleaf Law Publications, 2002), p. 6.
2. Ibid., p. 19.

3. Ibid., pp. 1-2.

4. Ibid., pp. 244-245.

5. See, for example, Nancy G. La Vigne and Julie Wartell, *Mapping across Boundaries* (Washington, D.C.: Police Executive Research Forum, 2001).

6. Peter Drucker, *Management Challenges for the Twenty-first Century* (New York: HarperCollins, 1998), pp. 102-103.

7. Jeanne W. Ross, Peter Weill, and David C. Robertson, *Enterprise Architecture as Strategy* (Boston: Harvard Business School Press, 2006), p. vii.

8. Ibid., pp. 195-199.

9. Stephen Baker, *The Numerati* (Boston: Houghton Mifflin, 2008).

10. Ben Worthen, "Mining for Gold," *Wall Street Journal*, October 27, 2008, p. R-9.

11. Karl Albrecht, *The Northbound Train* (New York: AMACOM, 1994), pp. 73-78.

12. Ibid., pp. 111-118.

13. Karl Albrecht, *Corporate Radar* (New York: AMACOM, 2000), pp. 49-68.

14. Karl Albrecht, "Organizational Intelligence and Knowledge Management: Thinking Outside the Silos," available at Karl.Albrecht.com; and Albrecht, "The Triune Intelligence Model: An Optimist View of Human Capability" (rev. June 2008), available at the same website.

9.

. . . .

USING CONSULTANTS

. . . .

If you deal with risk of any type, it is likely you have used or will use consultants at some point. There are perhaps almost as many consultant jokes as there are lawyer jokes, but a good consultant, if carefully selected and properly used, can be worth her weight in gold. To accomplish this, it helps if you understand how consultants see the world and how they operate.

Consultants are, by and large, subject-matter experts (SMEs). Through education, training, and experience, they can bring to the table a range and depth of knowledge beyond that usually found within a given corporation. In addition, they have the advantage of being outsiders. They are not confined by the social relationships present within the corporation, nor are they afraid (if they are good) to challenge the prevailing conventional wisdom. They also bring a fresh set of eyes. They did not create or grow up with the issue now in question, so they can be dispassionate and objective when viewing it.

Having said that, I should add that we should spend some time understanding consultants' business model, what they can and cannot do, and how they operate. Most of what they offer is positive, but some of it, not properly understood or recognized, can be negative.

➢ **Define objectives.** By the time you get to the point of considering the retention of a consultant, you have a pretty firm idea in mind as what the issue is. Your idea may be accurate or it may be wrong—perhaps not totally so, but wrong nonetheless. Here is a case in point. A number of years ago, I had a potential client call. It was from the director of internal audit for a company that manufactured and sold medical diagnostic devices. These were quite sophisticated machines that some doctors had in their offices to use when attempting to diagnose a patient's condition.

The company had a staff of salespeople who were trained to use the devices and to understand the maladies they were meant to help diagnose. At any given time, each salesperson had an inventory of about a dozen of these devices; if a salesperson could get a doctor interested in them, the salesperson would install one in the doctor's office for a test run of several months' duration. After that period of time, the salesperson was supposed to either complete a lease sale to the doctor, who was now convinced of the worth of the device, or retrieve it and put it back into inventory. There was, however, a caveat—the devices were quite complex and had to be returned to the manufacturer periodically to be tested and recalibrated.

The director of internal audit was now alarmed because a surprise inventory count had revealed that a number of the devices could not be accounted for—they were not in the salesperson's possession but had not been returned to inventory, and, since they were very expensive, the company was potentially out a lot of money. Evidently, this situation had existed for some time and the people in charge of inventory had been aware of it, but this was the first time the director of internal audit had learned of it. He feared the company had lost some very valuable machines.

I mentioned to him that the company had a much bigger potential problem. These machines were used to diagnose very serious medical problems, and the company had known for a good while that a number were missing. The supposition was that unethical sales personnel had either leased them or sold them to doctors and pocketed the money. The risk to the company, however, was infinitely larger than the missing machines. If a doctor misdiagnosed a patient because a machine was out of date and had not been properly recalibrated and the patient died, any good tort lawyer who learned of the machine's faulty performance and the company's prior knowledge of missing machines would have a field day. In such ways can consultants help better define a problem.

However, there is a word of caution. Some consultants have a tool, or a process, or a technique they have worked very hard on and perhaps even trademarked. It may be a very useful way to approach or manage a problem, if it is the right problem. But, there is an old saying: "If your only tool is a hammer, sooner or later everything begins to look like a nail."

Be cautious of consultants who try to shape your problem to fit their tool.

➤ **Determine qualifications**. You do not need a license to hang out your shingle as a "consultant." This is not an issue for larger corporations, as they tend to use the major professional services firms, but even then skill sets and abilities vary. It is important to know how your engagement will be staffed. Will the person, probably a partner or a partner equivalent such as principal, a director, or an executive director, who made the sales presentation to you also be the person who will be in charge of your engagement and, if so, what level of involvement will that person have? Except on truly large engagements (those well into the seven-figure range and up), it is likely this person will have other clients she is pitching work to or is managing work for. Determine the level of the principal's involvement and also determine the top on-scene person who will be running your engagement on a day-to-day basis. This may be a more junior partner or a senior manager. I suggest you meet with this person, with the partner hovering to protect the lower-level person, to assess his skill set, style, and understanding of your issues. This will be, after all, the person you and your people will have the most in-depth interaction with as the engagement moves forward.

➢ **Determine staffing.** If yours is a large engagement, there may be six or more people assigned to it. (I once ran one that had forty-six people assigned for a period of two and one-half years.) Staff personnel are usually young, bright, energetic, well-trained professionals in the early stages of their careers, but they also have a metric (we have discussed these in Chapter 2). It is called "utilization," and it refers to the number of hours out of a 2,000-hour work year that the person working on something is billable to a client. These younger folks watch these numbers like a hawk, since they are a big factor on their report card when it comes to compensation and promotion. They may be wrapping up one engagement when they are assigned to yours or, because of staff shortages, be working on two or more engagements at the same time, bouncing back and forth as need be. Also, because of their skill set, they may be pulled off your engagement to work on another and be replaced by someone who is new to your situation. Try to get as much clarity as you can as to how your engagement will be staffed and what the likely turn-over will be.

➤ **Define scope and budget.** Once the nature of the issue and the objective are agreed upon, it is normal for the consultant to produce a work plan. This will define personnel to be assigned, tasks to be performed, key milestones, timetables for delivery of reports, and budget. Often, clients want a firm budget up front. This can be dangerous, at least in the early stages. The consultant does not know how difficult the engagement is going to be—what level of support the consultant will receive from the client's staff, the condition of the client's hard copy and electronic data, and whether any additional issues will be uncovered during the course of the work. At the same time, the client does not want to sign a blank check for the consultant to do whatever she thinks is necessary, regardless of cost. This puts both parties in the position of making educated guesses as to what the scope and budget should be.

A useful way to deal with this issue, regardless of the nature of the work, is to do a "Phase One" approach. Both parties agree on a limited scope of work, a defined budget, a delivery date, and a report format. This can usually be done in a week or so. When it is completed, it gives both the client and the consultant a much better idea of what they are dealing with, what needs to be done, and how much it will cost.

➤ **Clarify and coordinate roles.** Make it clear who the consultant reports to. This may not be as simple as it sounds at first. Obviously, there is the person who hires the consultant, but then there is the person for whom the consultant is going to be working, and this may be a different person. Then there is the consultant's primary point of contact (POC), who will answer questions, expedite interviews and data collection, and so on. Then there is the person who will review and approve the consultant's invoices. These roles may be fulfilled by one person, or they may be fulfilled by four different people. If more than one person is involved in these roles, it is in everyone's best interests to ensure everyone is on the same page as to scope, budget, deliverables, and time frame.

➤ **Prepare for bad news.** Consultants do not actively seek bad news, but they seem to find it quite often. (See, for example, the case study discussed in Chapter 3 on the manufacturing company that thought it had one bad office, when it actually had twelve.) Using the fraud field as an example, in well over 75 percent of engagements the issue is larger than the client thought it was at the outset of the work. This often presents a bit of a Catch-22: often, the better the consultant does his work, the worse he makes the corporation and at least some of its executives look, since the problem happened on "their shift."

➤ **Determine the level of client support.** This is a common problem in consulting. The client promises, or the consultant infers, that a certain level of client support will be available to pull files, make copies of electronic data, participate in interviews, explain processes and procedures, and so forth. If this is not forthcoming one of two things happens, neither of which is good—the project slows down, affecting the delivery date, or the consultant uses his own people to do routine tasks, thereby driving costs up. There is nothing worse than a bunch of people sitting around a conference room table running up fees and wasting time because files that were supposed to be available when they got there at 8:30 A.M. still have not shown up by noon. It is a waste of the client's money, but consultants do not like it, either. It means they have to do their work quicker and cheaper to stay within budget or risk running over budget and having to explain to the client why it happened, which the client will not like. A little preparation on the client's part can go a long way to heading off this kind of problem.

   ➤ **Clarify administrative and travel costs.** It behooves you to get clarity on the handling of administrative and travel costs before the engagement begins. Some companies charge a flat percentage, say 10 percent, of professional fees for administrative overhead. This covers telephone calls, copying, and similar expenses incurred in the course of the engagement. I have, however, had clients who wanted such expenses itemized and justified in excruciating detail, such as "Make three copies of Johnson memo to Wilson regarding X matter, 22 pages each at $.065 per page, for review by Jones, Smith, and Banbridge." Requiring such detail is a double-edged sword. On the one hand, the client has a great amount of detail with which to question why a given expense was necessary (perhaps Smith really did not need to get a copy). On the other hand, the client is paying for this. Consultants, and their staffs, have only one thing to sell—their time. Many consultants charge for the time it takes to prepare such detailed reports or build the anticipated costs into the overall engagement budget.

So, too, with travel costs. The more clarity you can get up front, the better. How does the consultant charge for travel time? What class do the consultant and staff fly when they travel? What types of hotels do they stay in? Is there a per diem cap on meals and incidental expenses? Failure to understand and agree on such issues can burn up a lot of time later in discussions and arguments.

   ➤ **Clarify attorney work product privilege.** Using a consultant to deal with a risk is fine, but any risk issue carries with it another form of risk. The corporation may be in litigation over the issue, may be the object of a regulatory proceeding, or may be facing litigation and/or regulatory proceedings down the road. For this reason, many corporations choose to have the consultant retained by either their general counsel or their outside counsel. I am not an attorney, so please do not infer that I am offering legal advice. I am not qualified to do that. I am only reporting what I have encountered in the course of being involved in many risk-related engagements. Whether the consultant is retained by in-house counsel or outside counsel, she is still paid by the corporation. However, her communications regarding her work and findings must go to the attorney who hired her. Once they have been received, the attorney can, within reason, share them with whomever they believe needs to see them.

However, there are strict protocols around this procedure. All communications about the engagement, electronic or written, must carry a header. The one I have seen most frequently is:

PRIVILEGED AND CONFIDENTIAL
ATTORNEY WORK PRODUCT
PRELIMINARY DRAFT–FOR DISCUSSION
PURPOSES ONLY

To complicate matters further, the wording may change by jurisdiction. For example, several attorneys I worked for in New York State added the line:

PREPARED IN ANTICIPATION OF LITIGATION

The purpose of this disclaimer is to protect the client during discovery, that is, the sharing of documents that the other side can legitimately request to see during a legal or regulatory proceeding. The Attorney Work Product doctrine may provide some degree of protection, but this is an evolving body of law and may change from jurisdiction to jurisdiction. You are best advised to consult counsel regarding this issue.

➤ **Communicate.** Frequent communication is beneficial to both parties, as the client can learn how things are going, get a preliminary read on possible issues, and also see how the budget is holding up, and the consultant can advise of any issues that have come up in the execution of the work plan, including client personnel or data unavailability, that might impact budget or delivery dates and provide updates on any new or related issues that have come to light.

➤ **Never let a consultant work alone.** As noted, consultants are SMEs, and you should attempt to learn as much from them as possible. Structuring a work plan that closely involves client personnel has a number of benefits. The client team personnel have a much better grasp of the policies, procedures, and data resources of the corporation, can speed up the production of needed data, and can help explain the rationale behind various corporate practices. At the same time, client personnel can observe and interact with the consulting staff, pick up insights from them, and learn from experiences they have had with other clients. This creates a useful reservoir of knowledge that the client can access once the consultants have finished their work and may lessen the need to retain them again in the future.

10.

· ·

CONCLUDING THOUGHTS

· · · · · · · · · · · · · · · ·

Entering the world of risk feels like walking into Grand Central Station in New York City at the height of afternoon rush hour on a Friday. There are people everywhere, and they are all moving, and moving in different directions. Such is risk for the corporation.

WHO OWNS RISK?

One of the most difficult issues to deal with in this rush of activity is the most basic question: who owns risk? This, given the all-encompassing and changing nature of the question, is no small task. As attorney Ken Friedman notes, when things are going well, no one owns it, and, once trouble hits, everyone owns it. This sentiment is shared by risk professionals with decades of experience like those who were kind enough to provide interviews for this book (see Chapter 3) or who have written on the issue: Bill Parrett, former chairman of Deloitte & Touche LLP (D&T); Trent Gazzaway, head of the corporate governance practice for the multinational professional services firm Grant Thornton LLP (GT); Henry Ristuccia, head of the corporate governance practice for D&T; Dave Vannort, formerly of SCANA; and Skip Lange, a long-time consultant, among others. They all see risk ownership as a key, if slippery, issue that must be addressed if thoughtful progress is to be made; yet they acknowledge that it is not an easy task. The audit committee, the shareholders, and the employees on the shop floor all own some element or degree of risk, as is made clear by the current economic downturn in the world economy.

Yet, without a sense or declaration of ownership, how is action supposed to take place? If no ones clearly "owns" risk, are we not justified, to some degree, in following the great term Skip Lange coined—management by walking away? Certainly, in our daily and corporate lives, we face risks that are so normal and accepted that we no longer think of them much, as exemplified in the description of our daily routine of getting up and going to work. Yet, we live and operate in so dynamic and complex a corporate environment that the ability to merely keep track of risk becomes a risk in and of itself. If we miss something, that omission can have significant consequences.

This is the base question, and all corporations, great or small, would do well to ponder it, for without ownership there is no guidance and sponsorship, and without guidance and sponsorship there can be no action and strategy, and without action and strategy, there is no effort. And so we continue, as Karl Albrecht noted, to "advance until fired upon."

WHO IS RESPONSIBLE FOR RISK?

A subsidiary of the issue of ownership is responsibility. Assuming that the question of ownership has been defined or at least cleared up a bit, the responsibility for managing risk will likely fall to others, perhaps those high in the corporate hierarchy. The nine-step program used by D&T and set forth in the interview in Chapter 3 with Henry Ristuccia seems like both a logical and a comprehensive way to proceed. I am sure that other firms, like GT, have their own versions, but the message is clear—have a process to evaluate and understand risk, prioritize it, and have a coherent approach to managing it, with clear roles, responsibilities, and monitoring. Otherwise, you will be left with piecemeal, ad hoc, knee-jerk responses to whatever happens to pop up this week. Far too many companies operate in this mode and run the risk that one day the "pop" will be an explosion (witness the fate of the peanut-processing plant, discussed earlier).

Perhaps the greatest risk of all is making incorrect assumptions about risk.

"Wave theory" is a term common in several disciplines. Its premise is simple. Issues tend to behave like waves—they build, peak, and subside, then repeat the cycle. In organizations, we are usually in the position of chasing the last wave. We normally do not become aware of it until it is large and easy to see; then we begin to chase it with whatever remedies we believe will be effective; then we repeat the process when we sense the presence of the next wave. Much has been made of this tendency in the military (recall the comment that "generals are always prepared to fight the last war"). The process reminds one of Albrecht's story (see Chapter 4)—we advance, we are fired upon, we respond, we advance, and so on ad infinitum.

I fully endorse the study of what has happened—which I refer to as incident analysis—to detect patterns, trends, and hot spots. Perhaps more waves come from one area than another, and addressing those areas may reduce their size and frequency. We should not, however, rely solely on history to guide us into the future. My colleague, Dr. Daven Morrison, summed this up well in recounting an observation once made by one of his associates: "Preparing for the future by looking at the past is like steering a boat by looking at its wake."

To embrace the use of Trent Gazzaway's term "balance," we must be like the Roman god Janus, simultaneously looking both toward the past and toward the future to more fully understand our risk environment. And, to use a term used earlier, we should also "look sideways" to see what others are doing and what successes or failures they have experienced.

We may benefit from Dave Vannort's approach at SCANA, where executive management "drove" the responsibility for managing risk to the senior vice presidents by making them responsible for training their people and for implementing risk management strategies.

STAYING FOCUSED

Risk is such a large, varied, and complex issue that we sometimes have difficulty defining it. This can affect even how we discuss it, as there are so many potential views and angles on the subject. Many years ago, I had a very wise professor who described how discussions develop and end, as depicted in the following diagram.

We start with a fairly straightforward issue but, as the discussion proceeds, begin to branch out into related and similar issues. Eventually, at the point of maximum dispersion, there is a need to bring focus back to the discussion (perhaps because of time constraints or because there are now too many issues on the table to reasonably handle), and we wind down toward a close, trying to return to the original topic as best we can.

Such a phenomenon pretty much describes every discussion I

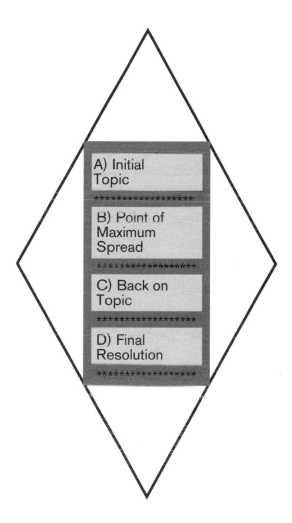

A) Initial Topic

****

B) Point of Maximum Spread

****

C) Back on Topic

****

D) Final Resolution

****

have ever been in, and it can be a danger when dealing with a topic so large, varied, complex, and interrelated as risk. There is a premium on staying focused, lest we wander around the realm of risk forever without defining issues and taking concrete action.

OPEN DISCUSSION

As noted elsewhere in this book, the mere discussion of risk can be risky in and of itself. In making a frank assessment of the risk a department, unit, or division faces, we may be seen as "confessing" our failings as a manager or an executive or be perceived as criticizing higher-ups for not taking more decisive action or not providing sufficient resources. This, obviously, can stifle discussion and produce a skewed and, therefore, flawed risk analysis.

Jeffrey Carr, vice president, general counsel, and Secretary of FMC, a manufacturer and supplier of technology and equipment, observes that creating an environment in which any participant is immune from negative implications from discussing risk "results in an open and frank discussion where we truly can disregard rank and not have to worry about offending our superiors."[1]

His observation speaks for itself if we really want to know what is going on in our risk environment.

WHEN IN DOUBT, MONITOR; WHEN NOT IN DOUBT, MONITOR

As has been noted throughout this book, many examples of risk in general are illustrated by fraud risk in particular. Barry Webne was convicted and sentenced to prison in 1997 for his embezzlement of $1.25 million from a medium-size manufacturing company he worked for in Cleveland. In 2006, he provided an interview to ACFE to discuss his activities. His comments are worth paying attention to as we think about risk of all types: "There was no oversight. . . . I think the company I worked for was typical of American companies. They left everything up to me as long as the financial statements were good—as long as the financial statements were turned in on time, nobody bothered us. . . . Nobody paid attention to the accounting department. We were worried about getting parts out the door, not whether inventory was stated correctly."[2]

Webne took money for his own use, and he notes that he started small and, when undetected, grew more daring. So, too, with all risk management systems. People have reports to file, numbers to accumulate, and the like. They need not be stealing to be tempted to cut corners or to report false numbers. Remember the property casualty company with bad numbers on claims closed; the credit card company with bad numbers on bad debt write-offs; the wholesaler with bad numbers on profitability; and the equipment manufacturer with bad numbers on the actual sales price of its equipment.

The human tendency to "fudge," if not steal, can also produce bad numbers in risk control and management systems. It may be the number of times a peanut-processing machine was cleaned, or it could be the manner in which a jet engine was removed for inspection and service—the bad results are the same.

As Trent Gazzaway observed, controls can erode with time.

DON'T OVERDO IT

Like anything, it is possible to overdo the amount of attention paid to risk. South Korea provides an example. Each November, a fair portion of South Korea shuts down: many offices and the stock market open an hour later than normal; most students get the day off; planes cannot land or take off from national airports; aircraft coming from other countries are instructed to circle at 10,000 feet to avoid noise; the Korea Electric Company puts 4,000 workers on standby for power emergencies and tests roughly 1,000 power lines, then leaves an engineer to monitor each individual line all day; 400 teachers and professors chosen by the government to prepare and review test questions are sequestered under armed police guard for weeks and are forbidden to use cell phones and the Internet; a motorcycle policeman races through the streets with lights flashing and siren blaring to retrieve a pass forgotten by a student; and more than 1,000 parents attend an overnight service in a temple where it is required that they, from a kneeling position, bow until the forehead touches a cushion on the floor. This is done 3,000 times.

It is the national day of testing for students in their final year of high school, and the results will determine which colleges they can attend. More than 80 percent of South Korean high school students go on to college, and the test day is, obviously, taken very seriously.[3]

The South Koreans are certainly entitled to their concerns and customs about the educational future of their children, but a corporation cannot come close to matching this level of precaution.

Understanding, continuously assessing, and monitoring risks ensures the deployment of resources to the highest priority areas without spending exorbitant amounts.

REMEMBER THE WINDOW AND ALSO "FAST EDDIE"

The "window" test from Chapter 5 helps remind us all of the temptation to assume, as do Fast Eddie's injunction to clear your mind (Chapter 3) and the statistics on doctors who interrupt their patient's descriptions of their symptoms after eighteen seconds. Assumptions are one of the most normal things in the world, but they can blind us to risk.

The law enforcement "cold case" concept has, of late, achieved some prominence in books, television shows, and movies, and it is real. It has been around law enforcement for decades, and there is a reason—it works. An initial investigator or team of investigators may be highly experienced and hardworking, but they may have missed something or, even more likely, have made an assumption. Having a fresh set of eyes take over has often produced surprisingly good results. So, too, with our thoughts and assumptions about risk. A fresh look every now and then may be a good thing.

BAD "BASELINES" AND RISK AS AN OLD FRIEND

No matter how intelligent we may be, there is sometimes a tendency to begin to learn to live with things that are not quite right or as right as we would like them to be. But, like the untreated scratch on the fender or the stain on the carpet, we see them so often they become part of the environment and, in so doing, become invisible. Having sold a few homes in my time, I am sometimes shocked and offended by what real estate agents see as flaws in my property that should be addressed before the house could attract the eye of a potential buyer. Like using a consultant, having a second set of eyes can be enlightening. We like to think of ourselves as careful stewards of the trust placed in our care, but, as Skip Lange noted, "management by walking away" can be an all-too-human impulse.

FORENSIC ACCOUNTANTS

Technically, a forensic accountant is one whose work may be used in a civil or criminal court proceeding. In common usage, the term refers to one who investigates possible frauds, but even this more casual term is misleading, for most often such investigations are done by two or more people, not one. The normal pairing is to have a forensic investigator and a forensic accountant work together. Some accountants have the requisite investigative skills and experience to work on their own, but they are more often the exception than the rule.

I have been asked often to explain forensic accounting, and I like to use the following: "An investigator starts with the people and moves toward the numbers. An accountant starts with the numbers and moves toward the people. They meet in the middle."

As with the example of the investor group with the last-minute warning that the books had been cooked, I started with the people and found two who were aware of the activity and willing to talk about it. Then the accountants took over and documented what had been done.

The model works very well, but it bespeaks a larger issue. Rarely is corporate risk the sole province of one skill set. It is not an accounting issue, or an IT issue, or a management issue. It is all of those things, and the wise corporation will craft a solution to address risk's many facets.

DEVELOPING RISK INTELLIGENCE

Writing in *GRC 360* magazine, Russell A. Jackson delivered a succinct but powerful appraisal of what is wrong with the manner in which many corporations approach risk-related issues. He cautions that:

- ➢ Being risk-aware without necessary context does not help manage risks.
- ➢ Only context can turn awareness into an effective risk management plan.
- ➢ Risk data without context are just additional data and do not facilitate decision making.[4]

Developing actionable intelligence is a function of awareness, full use of the organization's existing data, environmental scanning,

executive awareness and support, and continuous monitoring. Without such intelligence, we may produce much activity and many data
but not effectively manage much risk.

GO WITH YOUR GUT (OR SOMEONE ELSE'S)

We tend to discount our gut instincts as an oddity of human nature.
At the outset of this book, I tried to emphasize the value of human
beings as sources of useful intelligence, just as I tried to lay out some
of the lessons learned in law enforcement that might be applicable
in the corporate environment.

In law enforcement, there are people called "gun cops" or "dope
cops." These are the patrol officers and detectives who can sense
that something is wrong or that, in police terms, someone is "dirty."
They can do this with a casual glance while riding down the street,
and, more times than not, they are right. Many arrests have been
made this way, but a word of caution is in order. A hunch or a
suspicion is not probable cause for an arrest, but it may be enough
of an indicator for the officer to pull over and ask the person an
innocuous question, such as "Hey, buddy, how are you doing?" or
"Haven't I seen you before?" The person's responses and behavior
may then, in and of themselves, begin to provide probable cause. If
the person takes off running, that is a sure clue, as we say in the
business.[5]

The ability of some officers in every department and agency to
do this kind of law enforcement is well known and part of law enforcement lore, but the FBI decided to begin to study it: how was
this ability developed, how often was it effective, could it be taught?
The study is still ongoing, but the concept is interesting. In every
corporation, there are people who have a knack for seeing things

others do not, for finding problems that others are unaware of or have grown accustomed to being around. These people might be valuable team members when thinking about risk.

PROCESS VERSUS CRISIS

As I write this, the United States and most of the world are in an economic "crisis." Beware, for "crisis," while dire, can be a seductive word. Very few "crises" last 100 years, much less several thousand. By definition, "crisis" is an event bounded by time. It is unusual. It demands to be addressed. But, once these things happen, we can relax and declare the "crisis" to be "over." Risk identification and risk management are never over. Lest we believe so, review a small sample of magazine article titles from about two decades ago:

> "Crime? Greed? Big Ideas? What Were the '80's About?"[6]
> "For Wall Street Pros, Lying Comes Easily"[7]
> "The New Crisis in Business Ethics"[8]

Until we accept the basic proposition that risk assessment and management are part of a process, much like brushing our teeth and closing the door behind us, we are vulnerable to risk. Sudden surges do not work—brushing our teeth for six hours one day or closing our door 500 times over several hours does not insure us against risk for the next three months.

That is the seduction of a "crisis" mentality. We yearn to say, "Well, at least that's over."

It is not. It never will be. That is the way of the world. It both persists and evolves.

The blog Ghost in the Machine reports that the e-mail of the

U.S. Secretary of Defense was hacked into, the U.S. State Department lost terabytes of information, and both the Department of Homeland Security and the National Aeronautics and Space Administration suffered serious foreign cyberattacks.[9]

A report indicates that nearly two-thirds of high school students have cheated on tests and that most have also lied to their teachers. One-third used the Internet to commit plagiarism, and 82 percent have copied the work of another student. Interestingly, 26 percent said they had lied on at least one question when completing this survey on cheating and lying, yet 93 percent described themselves as having good ethics.[10]

Risk persists. Those who manage it prudently will survive. Those who do not will likely perish.

J. W. "Bill" Marriott once noted that it is often harder to stay on top than to get there. His words are memorable: "Success is never final."[11]

This is a good thing to remember about risk.

Robert J. Samuelson, in his *Newsweek* column "Judgment Calls," refers to this when he notes that we "want problems with instant solutions . . . victories and defeats with clear heroes and villains . . . a world of crisp moral certitudes, when the real world is awash with quirky ambiguities."[12]

Such is the nature of risk. Such is the nature of our challenge and our mandate—to use the cumulative experience we possess, the informed counsel of others, the technology at our disposal, our experience and wisdom, and the resources we have available to manage risk as best we can.

NOTES

1. Yesenia Salcedo, "Lessons Learned," *Inside Counsel* (September 2008), p. 48.

2. Scott Patterson, "Supposed 'Fraud' Consultant Charged with Another Embezzlement," *Fraud* (May–June 2008), pp. 14–15.

3. SungHa Park, "On College-Entrance Exam Day, All of South Korea Is Put to the Test," *Wall Street Journal*, November 12, 2008, p. A-1.

4. Russell A. Jackson, "Risk Intelligence," *GRC 360* (Fall 2008), p. 8.

5. Anthony J. Pinizzotto, Edward F. Davis, and Charles E. Miller III, "Intuitive Policing: Emotional/Rational Decision Making in Law Enforcement," *FBI Law Enforcement Bulletin* (February 2004), p. 1.

6. William Taylor, "Crime? Greed? Big Ideas? What Were the '80's About?" *Harvard Business Review* (January–February 1992), pp. 32–45.

7. Robert J. McCartney, "For Wall Street Pros, Lying Comes Easily," *Washington Post* (September 30, 1991), p. A-1.

8. Bruce Hager, "The New Crisis in Business Ethics," *Fortune* (April 20, 1992), pp. 167–176.

9. Center for Strategic and International Studies, "Securing Cyberspace for the 44th Presidency," quoted in "Ghosts in the Machine," *Atlantic* (March 2009), p. 17.

10. The Josephson Institute, "Report Card on the Ethics of American Youth," quoted in "Morality Bites," *Atlantic* (March 2009), p. 17.

11. Karl Albrecht, *The Northbound Train* (New York: AMACOM, 1994), p. 3.

12. Robert J. Samuelson, "Good Times Breed Bad Times," *Newsweek* (October 27, 2008), p. 55.

GLOSSARY

ABC: "apples, bushels, crop." A term first coined by Pete Anderson, a former federal prosecutor and now a private attorney in Charlotte, North Carolina, and later refined by Daven Morrison, a psychiatrist practicing in suburban Chicago. It refers to the question of whether a problem is caused by a "bad apple" executive or by a group of bad executives or whether the entire organization has problems.

ACFE: The Association of Certified Fraud Examiners, Austin, Texas. Founded in 1989 by former FBI special agent Joseph T. Wells and two colleagues, ACFE now has 50,000 members in more than 100 countries and is the largest, best-known, and most respected professional association devoted to the prevention, detection, and investigation of fraud.

AICPA: The American Institute of Certified Public Accountants. A professional and rule-setting body.

Background noise: False, inaccurate, obsolete, and/or misleading data included in a corporation's financial and other data systems so that effective management is hindered and the possibility of fraud or poor decisions is increased.

BCP: Business Continuity Planning. The process by which a corporation plans for the continuance of essential operations under a variety of risk scenarios.

BCSO: Brunswick County, North Carolina, Sheriff's Office.

Big Four: A term used to describe the four largest multinational professional services/accounting firms: Deloitte & Touche LLP; Ernst & Young LLP; KPMG LLP; and PricewaterhouseCoopers LLP.

"C suite": Generally, the top officers of a corporation, such as the chief executive officer, the chief financial officer, and the chief operations officer.

CEO: Chief Executive Officer. Generally, the top executive of any corporation.

CERT: Computer Evidence Response Team. Based at Carnegie-Mellon University, it investigates and researches various forms of computer-based misdeeds.

CFE: Certified Fraud Examiner. One who has passed a qualifications examination administered by ACFE and remains in good standing as a member of that organization.

COMPSTAT: A term referring to "computer statistics," a program begun by the New York Police Department in the mid-1980s to better track crime and other indicators of illegal activity. Widely used to deploy resources, adjust patrol patterns, and monitor field management performance, it is also a sometimes-grueling management philosophy. In various forms, it has been widely copied by other police departments.

Computer forensics: The use of computers and various analytical techniques to recover, search, and mine digital information. Usually used during investigations or in conjunction with litigation.

Corporate compliance: The process through a corporation tries to ensure that it is meeting the legal and regulatory requirements to which it is subject.

Corporate governance: The manner and process through which an organization, such as a corporation, seeks to manage its affairs and meet regulatory obligations.

COSO: The Committee of Sponsoring Organizations. A group formulated to recommend best practices for the conduct of corporate operations and affairs, especially with regard to compliance and governance.

CPA: Certified Public Accountant. In the United States, an accountant who has received additional training and passed qualifying examinations, qualifying the accountant to opine on various financial matters.

CPE: Continuing Professional Education. Similar to continuing legal education for attorneys. Many professions require that practitioners participate in a certain number of hours of education or other activities in a given period of time to maintain their professional standing.

CRO: Chief Risk Officer. Nominally, a high executive who is of stature equal to that of other "C suite" executives. At present, this position does not exist in many corporations, as risk has not been fully defined and made the responsibility of one person.

CSO: Chief Security Officer. A somewhat new, but spreading, title that pulls all corporate security functions (e.g., physical security, IT security, protection of IP) under one executive.

D&T: Deloitte & Touche LLP. A multinational professional services/accounting firm.

Diversion: See Gray market.

EOP: End of Period. In corporate financial operations, the end of a fiscal period. Typically, these occur once every three months and also once a year. For example, for a corporation that has a fiscal year that tracks the calendar year, there would be an EOP at the end of March, the end of June, the end of September, and the end of December. The EOP in December would also be the annual EOP.

ERM: Enterprise Risk Management. A definition often used is derived from a 2004 finding released by COSO (see entry) called "ERM: Integrated Framework." Basically, it sets forth recommendations for the most senior officials of an entity to identify risk and take prudent steps to address it in order to be able to achieve objectives.

FCPA: Foreign Corrupt Practices Act. A federal law that generally makes it illegal for any U.S. corporation or individual to bribe a foreign official for the purpose of getting business. The statute also requires that corporations keep sufficient records to allow the tracking of funds.

FSG: Federal Sentencing Guidelines. A set of rules and regulations promulgated by the U.S. Sentencing Commission to guide federal judges in the sentencing of individuals and corporations following their conviction.

GC: General Counsel. The top legal officer of any corporation. While the GC is the top official, a corporate legal department may have scores of other attorneys.

Ghost employee: A nonexistent employee put on the books of a corporation by a dishonest employee for the purpose of diverting the fictitious person's paycheck to the employee's use. The same technique is also used with "ghost vendors," where a nonexistent vendor is put on the books and paid, with the funds going to the benefit of a dishonest employee.

Gray market: Also called diversion or parallel pricing. When a company has a structured pricing system for its product(s), it may sell the same item for less in one country than another. The method used to take advantage of these discrepancies is to order as if from a low-cost country, then divert the product to a high-cost country, thereby profiting on the price differential. In some parts of the world, this is legal; in others, it is illegal.

GT: Grant Thornton LLP. A multinational professional services/accounting firm.

HRR: Holtz Rubenstein & Reminick LLP. An accounting and professional services firm based in the New York City area.

IC: The intelligence community. Agencies (almost all federal), such as the Central Intelligence Agency, the Federal Bureau of Investigation, the National Security Agency, and the National Reconnaissance Office, that provide the bulk of the intelligence "product" upon which the U.S. government bases its threat assessments.

IFP: Institute for Fraud Prevention. A not-for-profit group, funded by corporate contributions, that is currently administered by West Virginia University. IFP seeks to bring together scholars and practitioners from a number of fields to try to better understand, through discussion and sponsored research, what motivates fraud and how to better deal with it and ways to increase public awareness of its threat.

IP: Intellectual Property. Proprietary information held by an organization. It can range from patents and trademarks, to customer lists, marketing plans, and compensation levels.

IT: Information Technology. Roughly speaking, the use of computers and related systems to manage and interpret data.

Keyword search: In computer forensics, the process of interrogating a data file, usually belonging to a client, for keywords used in e-mails or written documents (e.g., "bribe" or "falsify") that may suggest improper activity.

LAN: Local Area Network. The linking of several computers so that they can share information or jointly work on tasks.

LCC: Low-cost countries. Those countries, typically in the Third World, that have abundant cheap labor.

MIS: Management Information Systems. A term widely used in corporations and organizations to refer to the computer infrastructure that collects, analyzes, and provides information needed by managers.

NYPD: The New York Police Department, the primary police agency in New York City.

Occupational fraud: The use of one's status as an employee to steal from one's employer.

Parallel pricing: See Gray market.

PC: A personal computer.

ROI: Return on Investment. A basic concept in business, it refers to the simple question "If I spend X, how much do I get in return?"

RTN: The annual report compiled by ACFE detailing the state of occupational fraud in the United States. It is free online at the ACFE website.

SAS: Statement of Auditing Standards. Promulgated by the American Institute of Certified Public Accountants, it provides guidance and sets out requirements for accountants and auditors. SAS 99, which deals with financial misstatements, became effective in December 2002.

SOX: An acronym for the Sarbanes-Oxley Act of 2002. A response to the Enron corporate accounting scandal, this act mandates significant changes in the rules of corporate governance and also the manner in which accountants' auditing corporations should operate.

Tone at the Top: The theory that corporate compliance and other objectives are best met by having top-level executives send clear signals about expected standards of behavior through their own behavior and methods of operation.

USSS: The U.S. Secret Service, an agency of the U.S. government usually associated with protecting the president and other high federal officials. It is also tasked with the investigation of various financial crimes, especially those committed by electronic means.

INDEX

Abagnale, Frank, 16, 110–112
ABC model, 59, 109–110, 223
accounting
    EOP manipulation in, 114–115
    forensic, 217–218
    inventive, 69–71, 178
ACFE, *see* Association of Certified
    Fraud Examiners
acquisitions
    and control/reporting systems, 25,
        100–102, 105–109, 113
    deal killers in, 97–98
ACs (audit committees), 82–83
actionable intelligence, *xiv,* 124, 195,
    218–219
actions, tone and, 85–87, 90
administrative costs, for consultants, 205
advance until fired upon philosophy, 77,
    210
AICPA, *see* American Institute of Certi-
    fied Public Accountants
Albrecht, Karl, 211
    on approaches to risk issues, 77, 210
    Eight Critical Environments concept
        of, 195–197
Albrecht, Steve, on fraud, 29

alert metrics (risk), 52
Alert Network, 191
Alison, Graham, 135
American Airlines, 104
American Institute of Certified Public
    Accountants (AICPA), 156, 224
Anderson, Peter, 109, 223
Andretti, Mario, 96
animals, risk perception by, 9–11
anonymous communications, 161, 166,
    173–174
apples, bushels, crop model, *see* ABC
    model
Apter, Michael, 30
The Art of the Steal (Frank Abagnale),
    111
Association of Certified Fraud Exam-
    iners (ACFE), 223, 229
    on control systems, 148–156
    on fraud, 20–26
    on perpetrators of fraud, 22, 24, 141,
        159
assumptions, 52–54, 141–145, 211–212,
    216–217
assurances, 128–129